The Mathematics Tuner for Certification of Elementary Educators

by Joseph Caruso

The contents of this work, including, but not limited to, the accuracy of events, people, and places depicted; opinions expressed; permission to use previously published materials included; and any advice given or actions advocated are solely the responsibility of the author, who assumes all liability for said work and indemnifies the publisher against any claims stemming from publication of the work.

Dorrance Publishing Co
585 Alpha Drive
Suite 103
Pittsburgh, PA 15238

Visit our website at *www.dorrancebookstore.com*

ISBN: 979-8-88729-254-0
eISBN: 979-8-88729-754-5

THE MATHEMATICS TUNER

FOR

CERTIFICATION OF

ELEMENTARY EDUCATORS

Over 1000 problems to help prepare for

an elementary education license

Answers for all problems are included

JOSEPH CARUSO

Table of Contents

INTRODUCTION

If your mind and heart is focused on becoming a K – 6 licensed elementary teacher, then *The Mathematics Tuner for Certification of Elementary Educators* with its over one-thousand problems is a resource that you should be without.

Creative problem solving, precise reasoning, effective communication, and alertness to the reasonableness of results are some of the essential problem-solving strategies that mathematics educators deem as necessary for all students to function effectively in their mathematics courses. It is the spirit of the aforementioned problem-solving strategies that *The Mathematics Tuner for Certification of Elementary Educators* is for future teachers in elementary grades.

The Mathematics Tuner for Certification of Elementary Educators is intended to help the future elementary educator become a better problem solver by exposing him/her to a wide variety of problems from the mathematical areas of Algebra, Number Theory, Geometry and Measurement, and Probability and Statistics. The problems presented in this exercise book are challenging, interesting and can easily be blended into the teaching styles and strategies of students and professors who are seeking supplementary problems that support and enhance the curriculum for the preparation of future elementary teachers.

The major academic areas selected in *The Mathematics Tuner for Certification of Elementary Educators* are typical of those found in the curricula of courses offered to elementary education majors in most college settings for the preparation of elementary teachers. All the problems presented in this exercise book can be used to enhance the student's problem-solving skill and techniques and provide an opportunity to delve into concepts that the student may be somewhat unfamiliar with.

As previously stated, the problems presented in *The Mathematics Tuner for Certification of Elementary Educators* could also be used by students to help them prepare for exams that are dedicated for the licensure of elementary teacher candidates. It is recommended that when problems are correctly solved, that other techniques for solving the same problem are explored so that students can expand their problem-solving skills, techniques, and strategies so that they might be applied to future problem-solving situations.

Mathematical thought along with the notion of problem solving is playing an increasingly important role in nearly all phases of human endeavor. The problems presented in *The Mathematics Tuner for Certification of Elementary Educators* should help provide the student with a mechanism to witness a variety of applications in a wide sphere of settings.

It is important to recognize that all problems in *The Mathematics Tuner for Certification of Elementary Educators* should be approached by putting the calculator aside and employ "pencil and paper solution". This approach for solving the problems presented in *The Mathematics Tuner for Certification of Elementary Educators* is consistent with emphasis by teacher licensing agencies to use a variety of problem-solving skills, techniques, and strategies to develop solutions to mathematics problems.

The Mathematics Tuner for Certification of Elementary Educators provides the teacher candidate with a variety of problems where the following dozen tools and techniques: (1) guess and check, (2) find a pattern, (3) visualizing, (4) work backwards, (5) reread the problem with your solution, (6) fix mistakes, (7) solve the equation, (8) identify important information and eliminate extraneous information, (9) make a list, (10) act it out, (11) be systematic, and (12) use known skills, could be used for successful and established approaches to problem solving.

In closing, teaching can be thought of as a mission or a task that you have been entrusted with. A teacher is expected to contribute to the betterment of his/her students in his/her own unique style and manner. As a teacher you will be in a position to influence every child you encounter and make them a better and a happier learner.

ALGEGRA

A001. At the Taxes Included Coffee Emporium, one cup of coffee and 3 doughnuts cost $3.90. Two cups of coffee and 2 doughnuts cost $4.32. What is the cost of one cup of coffee and one doughnut?

A002. If x and x – 3 are integers, what is the result, in terms of x, when the smaller integer is subtracted from 3 times the greater integer?

A003. Each day Richard earns $3 for doing certain chores. He can earn $5 instead by doing additional chores as well. After ten days of doing chores, Richard has earned a total of $36. On how many of these days did Richard do additional chores?

A004. What polynomial must be added to $7y^3 - 8y^2 - 13y + 21$ to get $3y^3 - 7y^2 + 15$?

A005. Simplify: $(x - x)(x^2 - x)(x^3 - x)(x^4 - x)(x^5 - x)$.

A006. Find the sum of the roots of: $3x^2 - 13x = 10$.

A007. The formula $M = \dfrac{P(rt + 1)}{12t}$ can be used to calculate the monthly payment M on a loan where P is the principal, r is the annual rate, and t is the length of the loan in years. Based on this formula, what is the monthly payment on a 2-year loan for $3000 at an annual rate of 8 %.

A008. If a car travels at a rate of 80 kilometers per hour without stopping, how many kilometers does it travel between 9:15 AM and 12:00 noon on the same day?

A009. Find x % of $\dfrac{1}{x}$.

A010. Find the line L that passes through the point (4, 9) and is perpendicular to the line: 4x + 3y = –6. Express line L in the form Ax + By = C.

A011. Multiply the reciprocal of a positive number by the opposite of that same number. The product will be:

A012. How many values of x satisfy: $\dfrac{x^2}{x - 2} - \dfrac{4}{x - 2} = 0$?

A013. Mary usually drives the 600 miles from Boston to Pittsburgh in 12 hours. If she increases her average speed by 10 miles per hour, how much time will the trip take?

A014. Solve for x: $2 + \dfrac{\dfrac{2^{-1} + 3^{-1}}{2}}{4 - \dfrac{2}{1 - \dfrac{1}{5}}} = \dfrac{1}{x}$

A015. For what values of x is: $\dfrac{3}{x} > \dfrac{4}{x}$, $x \neq 0$.

A016. Leah travels from city A to city B to city C and back to city A. Each city is 120 miles from the other two. Her average speed from A to B is 60 mph. Her average speed from B to C is 40 mph. Her average speed from C to A is 24 mph. Overall, what is Leah's average speed for the entire trip?

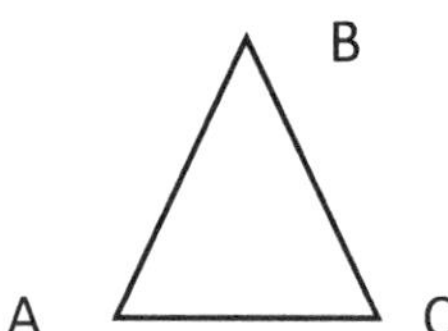

A017. If $x > 0$ and $x^2 - 2x + 1 = 100{,}000{,}000{,}000{,}000$, find x.

A018. If $4 + 2(3x - 4) = 8$, then $3x - 4$ equals:

A019. The difference between twice the larger number and three times the smaller number is 3. Three times the sum of the two numbers is 57. What are the two numbers?

A020. Find the line L that passes through the point (3, 5) and is parallel to the line: $2x - 3y = 12$. Express line L in the form $Ax + By = C$.

A021. If the cost, in dollars, of a high protein energy bar is the same as the number of different values of x which satisfy $(x^2 - 9)^3 = 0$, find the cost of this high protein energy bar.

A022. Find the equation if the roots are: $\dfrac{2}{3}$ and $-\dfrac{1}{4}$.

A023. Positive integers x and y have a product of 56 and $x < y$. 7 times the reciprocal of the smaller integer plus 14 times the reciprocal of the larger integer equals 4. Find x.

A024. A low wattage radio station is located 3 miles from an interstate highway. The station has a range of 6.1 miles in all directions from the station. If the interstate is along a straight line, how many miles of highway (correct to tenths) are in the range of the station?

A025. The Bertolucci family raises both sheep and chickens on their farm. In total their farm animals have 23 heads and 70 legs. How many chickens do they have?

A026. Five years ago, Mike's age was three times Linda's age. In two years, Mike's age will be two times Linda's age. How old is Linda now?

A027. Solve for x: $3^x + 4^x = 2$.

A028. A line passes through the points (−1, 6), (6, k), and (20, 3). Find k.

A029. A store that sells handcrafted items takes $3.00 per item plus 40% of the sale price for each item sold. The remainder of the money from the sale price goes to the craftsperson. If P represents the sale price of one item, find an expression in terms of P for the amount of money, C, that a craftsperson earns for each item sold.

A030. Solve for C: $\dfrac{1}{x-1} - \dfrac{1}{x+1} = \dfrac{C}{x^2-1}$.

A031. If a board 25 inches long is cut into two pieces so that one piece is 7 inches shorter than the other, what is the length of the shorter piece?

A032. Simplify: $1 + \dfrac{y}{x+y} - \dfrac{x}{x-y}$.

A033. Five members of a riding club decide to buy a 10-speed mountain bike and agree to share the cost equally. Three new members join the club, and they agree to pay their fair share of the cost of this bike. This resulted in a savings of $15 for each of the original five members. What was the cost of this bike?

A034. Solve for x: $6^x + 6^x + 6^x + 6^x + 6^x + 6^x = 6^6$.

A035. The sum of two fractions is $\dfrac{11}{15}$. Three times the larger minus two times the smaller is $\dfrac{8}{15}$. Find the two fractions.

A036. If $r = 3^y - y$ and $y = 2^n + 1$. Find r when n = 2.

A037. If (a,b) and (c,d) are coordinates of different points on the graph of 3x + 4y = 5, find the value of $\dfrac{b-d}{a-c}$.

A038. If x + 3 = y, express x^2 + 6x + 9 in terms of y.

A039. Two integers differ by 4. The difference of their squares is 72. Find the integers.

A040. A certain math exam is scored by awarding 6 points for each correct response, 0 points for each incorrect response, and 1.5 points for each problem left unanswered. After looking over the 25 problems on the exam, Anna has decided to attempt the first 22 problems and leave only the last 3 unanswered. How many of the first 22 problems must Anna solve correctly in order to score at least 100 points?

A041. If the sum of two numbers is 20 and four times the larger exceeds three times the smaller by 143. Find the larger number.

A042. If $3x + \dfrac{3}{x} = 5$, find the value of: $3x^2 + \dfrac{3}{x^2}$.

A043. For how many different integer values of x is $\dfrac{2}{x}$ an integer?

A044. Gino leaves his house in Stoneham at noon and travels north at a constant speed of 32 mph. His wife Fran leaves the same house at 1:30 and travels at a constant speed of 44 mph. At what time does Fran catch up to Gino?

A045. How many minutes faster will Jake complete a 100-mile drive traveling at a rate of 65 mph than if he traveled at a rate of 55 mph. Express your answer to the nearest whole number.

A046. A driver completed a trip in 5 hours. If the average speed had been 12 kph faster, the trip would have taken one hour less. How many kilometers was covered by this driver?

A047. Emily has a collection of bicycles and tricycles. She has 36 pedals and 43 wheels. How many tricycles does Emily have?

A048. A school plans to sell T-shirts with the school's logo on them. The cost of each T-shirt alone is $3.50 and the printing cost for each T-shirt is 75¢. If the class plans on selling each printed T-shirt for $11, write an expression that can be used to calculate the profit for selling N T-shirts?

A049. For plumbing repairs in the home, Mr. Fixit charges \$15 an hour plus a service-call charge. After working 3 hours in a home, his bill came to \$58. How much does Mr. Fixit charge for a service-call?

A050. The owner of a house wants to convert a stairway leading from the ground to the back porch into a ramp. The porch is 3 feet off the ground and due to building regulations, the ramp must start 12 feet away from the base of the porch. Correct to tenths, how long will the ramp be?

A051. Sal leaves his house in Salem at noon and runs at a constant speed of 2 mph. His sister Val leaves the same house at 1 PM and runs after Sal at a constant speed of 3 mph. At what time does Val catch up to Sal?

A052. Simplify: $\left(3a^2 - 2a + 3 \right) \times \left(3a - 1 \right)$.

A053. Solve for x: $x^{-1}\left(\dfrac{3^{-1}}{2^{-2} + 3^{-2}} \right) = \dfrac{3}{4}$.

A054. If $(m - n)^2 = 4k^3$, and $2mn = 3k^3$, and $k \neq 0$, what is the value of $(m + n)^2$ in terms of k?

A055. Kathy is 3 times as old as Laura. Kathy's age is one-third of her father's age. If Laura is x years old, how old is Kathy's father in terms of x?

A056. If 100a + 100b = 1, find $\dfrac{1}{2}a + \dfrac{1}{2}b$.

A057. The sum of two numbers is 20. The sum of their squares is 300. Find the product of these two numbers.

A058. A normal duck has two legs. A lame duck has one leg. A sitting duck has no legs. Donald has 33 ducks. He has two more normal ducks than lame ducks and two more lame ducks than sitting ducks. How many legs in all do the 33 ducks have?

A059. Suppose $x = t^2 + t$ and $y = t^3 + t^2$. If x = 2, find all possible values of y.

A060. The sum of two fractions is $\dfrac{11}{15}$. Three times the larger minus two times the smaller is $\dfrac{8}{15}$. Find the smaller of these two fractions.

A061. Solve the system:

$$2x - y = 15$$
$$3x + 2y = 12$$

A062. Find D if $(x + 1)(x + 2)(x + 3)(x + 4) = (x^2 + 5x + 4)(D)$.

A063. The product of two numbers is 30 and their sum is 16. Express their positive difference in simplest radical form.

A064. How many hours will a car traveling at 45 mph take to catch up with a car travelling at 30 mph if the slower car starts two hours before the faster car?

A065. $P(x) = 2^x - 1$ where x is a prime number. What is the sum of the three smallest distinct values of $P(x)$.

A066. What is the sum of the values of x that satisfy: $9^{\left(x^2 - x - 30\right)} = 1$.

A067. The number of hours, h, it takes for a block of ice to melt varies inversely as the temperature. If it takes 2 hours for a square inch of ice to melt at 65°, how long, correct to minutes, will it take for the same size ice to melt at 95°?

A068. Joan and Sandy went to NH mall shopping where there is no sales tax. Joan bought four CDs and three audio books for $89. Sandy bought three CDs and two audio books $64. If all the CDs were the same price and the books on tape were the same price, what was the price of one CD?

A069. Anne plants a oak tree and she measures the height of the tree at the end of each year. The tree grows 7 inches during a rainy year and 4 inches during a dry year. After x years, the tree grew 84 inches. Find the sum of all possible values of x.

A070. Solve for x: $1 < 4x + 1 < 3$.

A071. Bob can run 1 mile in the same time that Phil can run $\dfrac{5}{6}$ of a mile. Cindy can run $\dfrac{3}{4}$ of a mile in the same time that Phil can run 1 mile. If each person runs at those rates, how many miles will Cindy run in the time it takes Bob to complete an 8-mile run?

A072. The weight of a body varies inversely as the square of its distance from the center of the Earth. If the diameter of Earth is 8000 miles, how much would a 200-pound man weigh 1000 miles above Earth?

A073. Find both integers n that satisfy: $n^2 + n^4 = 2^2 + 2^4$.

A074. The sum of two integers is 45. The sum of the quotients of these two integers is 2.05. Find the product of these two integers.

A075. If $m^2 - n^2 = 4k^3$, and m − n = 12k, and k ≠ 0, find m + n in terms of k.

A076. If a and b are the two roots of $x^2 - 5x + 3 = 0$, find (a + b)(ab).

A077. Traveling a certain route, the distance between Boston and New York City is 310 miles. A car starts from Boston at 1 PM and travels along this route towards NYC at a steady rate of 50 mph. Another car starts from NYC at 1:30 PM and travels along the same route towards Boston at a steady rate of 45 mph. At what time do the cars pass each other?

A078. Sarah has $30 to spend on one book at a bookstore's fund raiser. She has a coupon for 15% off the total cost of one book. She will also be charged 7% of the cost of the book for a local charity. What is the price (before she uses the coupon) of the most expensive book that Sarah can buy?

A079. If x + y = 201, and $\dfrac{1}{x} + \dfrac{1}{y} = 201$, what is the value of xy?

A080. The Tracy Tire Company produces tires for cars and motorcycles. During a 5 day period, the company produced 269 tires for 70 vehicles. This included a spare tire for each car but not for any motorcycle. How many motorcycle tires did Tracy Tire produce during that 5 day period.

A081. Barney and Helen are flying to Washington DC. They each bring 2 suitcases on the trip. One of Barney's suitcases weighs 6 pounds more than Helen's heavier suitcases. His other suitcase weighs 7 pounds more than Helen's heavier suitcase. Helen's lighter suitcase weighs 3 pounds less than her heavier suitcase. The total weight of all 4 bags is 110 pounds. How much does Barney's heavier suitcase weigh?

A082. Two times the first integer minus the second integer equals 5. Three times the first integer minus two times the second integer equals −6. Find the two integers.

A083. Given line L: x + y = 7 and line M: 5x − 3y = 11. Find the point of intersection of L and M.

A084. In the coordinate plane, find the distance between (3, 5) and (–5, 20).

A085. Erika has three kinds of cycles in her shop: unicycles, bicycles, and tricycles. There are a total of 150 wheels and 70 seats in Erika's shop. There are twice as many bicycles as tricycles. How many of each kind are in Erika's shop?

A086. Solve for x: $x^{-1}\left(\dfrac{3^{-1}}{2^{-2} + 3^{-2}} \right) = \dfrac{3}{4}$.

A087. Solve for A: $\dfrac{x + 2}{x + 1} = 1 + \dfrac{A}{x + 1}$.

A088. Find the greatest possible value of x given: $\left(\dfrac{4x - 16}{3x - 4} \right)^{2} + \dfrac{4x - 16}{3x - 4} = 12$.

A089. Sarah rode her bike at the rate of 12 mph for $3\dfrac{1}{2}$ hours. If her brother Michael rides for 3 hours, at what average speed would he have to ride his bike to travel the same distance?

A090. The product of two numbers is 108 and the sum of the two numbers is 24. What is the positive difference between these two numbers?

A091. Solve for x: $9 - 5(3 - 2x) = 4(2 - x)$.

A092. Factor completely: $6x^{3} + 25x^{2} + 4x$.

A093. A box contains $2.25 in nickels and dimes. There are three times as many nickels as dimes. Determine the number of nickels and dimes in the box.

A094. Solve the system: $\begin{aligned} \dfrac{1}{x} + \dfrac{2}{y} &= 6 \\ \dfrac{2}{x} - \dfrac{1}{y} &= 7 \end{aligned}$

A095. In a chess match, a win counts 1 point, a draw counts one-half point, and a loss counts zero points. After 15 games, the winner was 4 points ahead of the loser. How many points did the loser have?

A096. If $x^2 + 2x = 46$, what is the value of $x^4 + 4x^3 + 4x^2 + 66$.

A097. At an amusement park, Kay was charged $12.90 for 5 go-cart rides and 3 roller-coaster. Allie paid $16.80 for 10 go-cart rides and 1 roller-coaster ride. Their friend Nicole would like to buy as many roller-coaster rides as possible with her $20 bill, how much money will she have left over?

A098. Solve for x: $2 - \dfrac{2x - 1}{3} = \dfrac{7 - 3x}{5}$

A099. Solve for x: $3^{2x-1} = 1$.

A100. The least common multiple of $x^2 - 4$ and $x^2 - 4x + 4$ is:

A101. Solve for x: $7x^2 = 21x$.

A102. Solve for x: $1 + \dfrac{1 - \dfrac{3}{8}}{1 + \dfrac{2\frac{2}{3}}{1 - \dfrac{3}{5}}} = x^{-1}$.

A103. Find the vertex of $y = x^2 + 12x + 35$.

A104. If $ab = 4$, $bc = 5$, $ac = 10$, find $a^2 + b^2 + c^2$.

A105. Solve for x: $3 + \dfrac{2 - \dfrac{3}{4}}{2 + \dfrac{1}{\frac{2}{3}}} = \dfrac{2}{x}$.

A106. The sum of the first and third of three consecutive integers is 131 less than three times the second. Find the integers.

A107. For the first half of a bike trip Joe road downhill at 24 mph for 2 hours. During the second half of the trip, he rode uphill at one-half his downhill speed for twice as long before returning to his starting point. What was Joe's average speed in mph for the entire trip?

A108. Mary has (m + 17) apples, Scott has (m + 8) apples, and John has (m + 5) apples. All of these apples are put into 3 empty boxes so that each box contains exactly x apples. What is the value of x in terms of m?

A109. Find the vertex of $F(x) = x^2 - 8x + 7$.

A110. M varies jointly as the values of p and q. If M = 88 when p = 4 and q = 0.4. Find M when p = 8 and q = 1.2.

A111. Given $f(x) = \dfrac{1}{3}x^2 + 2$. Find $f(a - 3)$.

A112. Solve for x: $2n - p = \dfrac{a}{x}$

A113. Find the quadratic function in the form of $y = x^2 + bx + c$ that passes through (−3, 9) and (8, 20).

A114. Solve for x: $\left(\dfrac{1}{27}\right)^{4-x} = \left(\dfrac{1}{81}\right)^{2x+3}$.

A115. Find the line in the form $y = mx + b$ that passes through (3, −2) and (−5, 6).

A116. If x is inversely proportional to y and $x = 4\sqrt{3}$ when y = 3. Find y when $x = 2\sqrt{3}$.

A117. Solve for x: $2 + \dfrac{x+4}{4} = \dfrac{3x+1}{7}$.

A118. One-sixth of a number plus one-seventh of a number is eight less than one-half of the number. Find the number.

A119. Find the positive integers (x, y) that satisfy 3x + 4y = 25.

A120. Find F if $x^3 - 1 = (x - 1)(F)$.

A121. A UPS driver who is paid by the hour earned $450 one week. If his hourly rate had been $3 more, he would have earned the same amount by working 5 hours less. What was his hourly rate of pay?

A122. Green cab charges $6 plus 28¢/mile for a ride. Yellow cab charges $8 plus 24¢/mile for a ride. How many miles must be driven by green cab to be more expensive than Yellow Cab?

A123. If ab = 2, then simplify: $\left(a - \dfrac{1}{b} \right) + \left(b - \dfrac{1}{a} \right)$.

A124. Solve for B in the equation $A = \left(\dfrac{h}{2} \right)(B + b)$.

A125. Solve for x: $\sqrt[6]{x} = \sqrt[3]{5^2}$.

A126. Two pounds of pears and one pound of peaches costs $1.40. Three pounds of pears and two pounds of peaches costs $2.40. How much is the combined cost of one pound of pears and one pound of peaches?

A127. If y varies directly as x and y = 9 when x = 2, what is y when x = −3?

A128. A rabbit and a turtle had a race. They started at the same time and place. When the turtle had gone only one-fourth the distance to the finish line, the rabbit had run to the finish line and back to the turtle. The rabbit ran __________ times as fast as the turtle.

A129. If P is inversely proportional to w and P = $\dfrac{2}{3}$ when w = $\dfrac{1}{4}$, what is P when w = $\dfrac{1}{6}$?

A130. Find the vertex of $y = x^2 - 10x + 21$.

A131. Solve for x: $\dfrac{3}{2}x + \dfrac{1}{3} = \dfrac{1}{4}x - \dfrac{1}{6}$.

A132. A varies jointly as L and W, and A = 30 when L = 3 and W = $5\sqrt{2}$, what is A when L = $2\sqrt{3}$ and W = $\dfrac{1}{2}$?

A133. Solve for x: $(3)^{-1}\left(\dfrac{x^{-1}}{4^{-1}+5^{-1}}\right)=4$.

A134. Huey's age plus Dewey's age equals 26. Dewey's age plus Louie's age equals 32. Huey's age plus Louie's age equals 28. Find their ages.

A135. A flagpole broke in a storm and 7 meters are still sticking straight out of the ground, where it snapped, but the remaining piece has hinged over and touches the ground at a point 24 meters away horizontally. How tall was the flagpole before it broke?

A136. The age of a man is the same as his wife's age with the digits reversed. If the sum of their ages is 99 and the man is 9 years older than his wife, how old is he?

A137. At the Boone Middle School, the first class starts at 8:26 AM and the fourth class ends at 11:26 AM. There are 4 minutes between classes and each class is the same length of time. How many minutes are there in one class?

A138. In a multiplication example, **A8** X **3B** = **2730**. Different letters represent different digits. Find the value of **A** and **B**.

A139. Hannah has a bag containing quarters and dimes. If she has 18 coins for a total of $2.40, how many dimes and quarters does she have?

A140. Three-fifths of the students in a class are women. If the number of men in the class were doubled and the number of women in the class were increased by 9, there would be an equal number of men and women in the class. How many men and women were originally in the class?

A141. Find the points where $x-y+9=0$ and $y=x^2+2x-3$ intersect.

A142. If 7X = 2Y and 3Y = 5Z, then 21X = ? Z .

A143. A certain family has 3 children. Mo's age plus Curly's age add to 20 years. Curly's age plus Larry's age add to 29 years. Mo's age plus Larry's age add to 23 years. Which child is between the oldest and youngest? What is the difference in age between the oldest and youngest?

A144. Solve for x: $2^{-2}\left(\dfrac{3^{-1}+x^{-1}}{3^{-1}-5^{-1}}\right)=3$.

A145. Both the numerator and denominator of $\dfrac{5}{4}$ are increased by 2. What is the positive difference between the new fraction and the original?

A146. A guy wire is attached to a telephone pole. The distance from the point where the wire touches the ground to the base of the telephone pole is 4 feet less than the length of the wire. How far up the telephone pole is the wire attached if the distance from the ground to where the wire is attached to the pole is 2 feet less than the length of the wire?

A147. Let $Y = Cp^{x}$ represent an exponential model for points (1, 6) and (3, 24). C and p are positive numbers. Find C + p.

A148. In a spelling bee, 50% of the students were eliminated after the first round. Only $\dfrac{1}{3}$ of the remaining students were still in the contest after the second round. If 24 students were still in the contest after the second round, how many students began the contest?

A149. The product of four consecutive positive integers is 1 less than 461^{2}. What is the least of these integers?

A150. A box of tacks weighs 120 g when full and 70 g when half full. How many grams does the box weigh when it is empty?

A151. When a positive integer is divided by 7 the remainder is 4. When the same integer is divided by 9, the remainder is 3. What is the smallest possible value of this integer?

A152. Including an $8\dfrac{1}{3}\%$ sales tax, a sofa costs %6500. What was the original cost of this sofa?

A153. The product of two whole numbers is 48. The average of the two numbers is 8. Find the larger of these two numbers.

A154. Solve for x: $8^{3x-1}=4^{x+2}$.

A155. At noon an airplane leaves Bedford Airport traveling north at 240 mph. At 3 pm, a jet leaves the same airport and follows the same path as the airplane but travels at a speed of 600 mph. how many hours will the airplane be flying before it is overtaken by the jet?

A156. A school's service club has six members. Two of them help the headmaster's office each school day. What is the greatest number of school days that can pass without repeating the same pair of students?

A157. Three-fifths of the students in a class are women. If the number of men in the class were doubled and the number of women in the class were increased by 9, there would be an equal number of men and women in the class. How many men and women were originally in the class?

A158. Al and Bill are playing a game. At a certain point in the game, if Al were to lose 2 of his chips to Bill, they would have the same number. If Bill were to lose 2 of his chips to Al, Al would have twice as many as Bill. How many chips does Al have just before either of these possible exchanges?

A159. A barrel full of flour weighs 40 pounds. The same barrel filled with nails weights 64 pounds. If the nails weigh three times as much as the flour, how much does the empty barrel weigh?

A160. Solve for x: $4 + 3(x - 5) = 7(x - 2)$.

A161. Solve for x: $\dfrac{2}{3}x - 4 = 5 + \dfrac{3}{4}x$.

A162. Solve for x: $7 - 5(x + 4) < 8 - 3x$.

A163. Solve for x: $\dfrac{5 - x}{3} \leq -2 + \dfrac{x}{2}$.

A164. If $f(x) = x^2 - 3$, find $f\left(\dfrac{1}{4}\right)$ in simplest rational form.

A165. Two cars leave the same parking lot, with one heading north and the other heading east. After some time elapses, the northbound car has traveled 40 km, and the eastbound car has traveled 96 km. Measured in a straight line, how far apart are the two cars?

A166. A cell phone plan gives the user 300 minutes per month for a fixed charge of \$29.95. The user pays an extra 35¢ per minute for all minutes beyond 300. What would a person pay if 430 minutes of calls are made during a particular month?

A167. On a 100 cm measuring stick, from left to right, marks are made at 19, N, and 99 cm. The distance between the marks at N and 99 cm is three times the distance between the marks N and 19 cm. What number is N?

A168. Solve for x: $8^{3x-1} = 4^{x+2}$.

A169. Al, Cal, and Sal each have a number of Susan B. Anthony silver, one-dollar coins. Together Al and Cal have a value of \$20, Al and Sal have a value together of \$25, and Cal and Sal have together a total value of \$27. What is the total value of the coins that Al, Cal, and Sal have?

A170. Bryan can buy candy canes at 4 for 50¢ and can sell them at 3 for 50¢. How many canes must Bryan sell in order to make a profit of \$5.00?

A171. Together Jim and Bob weigh 357 pounds. Together Jim and Larry weigh 393 pounds. The combined weight of all three men is 565 pounds. How much do Bob and Larry weigh together?

A172. If $g(x) = 2x - 7$ and $h(x) = \dfrac{2x-1}{x+1}$, find $g\!\left(h\!\left(\dfrac{5}{3}\right)\right)$ in simplest rational form.

A173. Solve for the variable x: $27^{2-x} = 81^{x+1}$.

A174. Let $z = \dfrac{w^2 x^3}{y}$. If P equals the value of the expression that results when the positive numbers w, x, and y are each doubled in the expression for z. Then P is how many times z?

A175. If $(a)(b) = 8$, $(b)(c) = 10$, $(a)(c) = 180$, express the value of $(a)(b)(c)$ in simplest form.

A176. The speed of a stream is 3 km/hr. A boat travels upstream 12 km and then returns to its original position along the same route. If the speed of the boat in still water is 9 km/hr, what is the average speed of the boat for the entire trip. [*fyi: traveling downstream means to be moving with the speed of the stream*].

A177. Solve for x: $3\left|2x+3\right| = 15$.

A178. In a certain class, there are twice as many girls as boys. One-half of the boys and two-thirds of the girls are studying physics. What part of the entire class is studying physics?

A179. Find the ordered pair of real numbers (x, y) that satisfies: $7^x - 11y = 0$ and $11^x - 7y = 0$.

A180. Amber decided to spend a week of her summer vacation on Cape Cod. On Monday she drove from Pittsfield to Falmouth in $3\frac{1}{3}$ hours at an average speed of 55.8 mph. When she drove back on Sunday, traffic was much heavier, and the trip took 5 hours. What was Amber's average speed on the return trip?

A181. BG and GB represent two 2-digit numbers. If BG − GB = 18, what is the value of the expression B − G?

A182. Three-Fifths Bank offers two checking account plans. Plan A: has a monthly fee of $9 and a three-cent charge per check. Plan B: has a monthly fee of $5 and an eight-cent charge per check. Under what conditions is it less expensive to use Plan A?

A183. Solve for x: $2 + \dfrac{5}{1 + \dfrac{3}{2 - \dfrac{2}{5}}} = \dfrac{1}{x}$.

A184. Given $A = \dfrac{4}{B}$ and $B = 5 - \dfrac{2}{C}$. Find C in terms of A.

A185. If A = 1, B = -2, C = 3, D = -4, E = 5, F = -6, ... and Z = -26, find the value of the expressions:
A + B + C + D + ... + Z .

A186. If A = 1, B = -2, C = 3, D = -4, E = 5, F = -6, ... and Z = -26, find the value of the expressions:
A − B − C − D −. . . . − Z .

A187. The sum of three numbers is 103. The ratio of the first to the second is 3:5. The ratio of the second to the third is 6:11. Find the three numbers?

A188. Find x > 0 that satisfies $\left(x^{-1} + \sqrt{2} \right)\left(x^{-1} - \sqrt{2} \right) = 16$.

A189. Find the quadratic function in the form: $y = x^2 + bx + c$ that passes through $(-4, -16)$ and $(3, -9)$.

A190. Solve for x: $2 - \dfrac{2x-1}{3} = \dfrac{7-3x}{5}$.

A191. Solve for x given: $x^2 - 6x + 8 = 0$.

A192. Solve for x given: $x^2 + 4x - 12 = 0$.

A193. Solve for x given: $x^2 - 10x + 24 = 0$.

A194. Rosa spent $72 for 320 baseball cards. There were 40 "old-timer" cards. She spent twice as much for each "old timer" card as for each of the other cards. How much money did Rosa spend for all the 40 'old timer" cards?

A195. Find the sum of the solutions of $(x - 8)^2 = 2021^2$.

A196. Together John and Jess have 72 marbles. John gives Jess half his marbles and then 12 more. Jess now has three times as many marbles as John has. How many marbles did Jess have originally?

A197. Find the intercepts and the vertex of: $y = x^2 - 10x + 21$.

A198. −5 is a root of $x^3 + x^2 - 41x - 105 = 0$. Find the other two roots of this cubic equation.

A199. Find the intercepts and the vertex of: $y = x^2 + 2x - 24$.

A200. Find the intercepts and the vertex of: $y = x^2 + 12x + 35$.

A201. Solve for x: $2\left|3x - 1\right| = 8$

A202. If $(x + 3)$ is a factor of $x^3 + 8x^2 + x - 42$, find the other factors.

A203. Solve for x: $\dfrac{3}{1 + \dfrac{2}{3 - \dfrac{1}{3}}} = \dfrac{1}{x}$.

A204. Solve for x: $2n - p = \dfrac{a}{x}$

A205. If Y is inversely proportional to X and Y = 8 when X = $\dfrac{2}{3}$. Find Y when X = 6.

A206. Solve for x: $\dfrac{1}{5x} - \dfrac{1}{4x} + \dfrac{1}{3x} = -\dfrac{17}{60}$.

A207. Solve for x: $2 + \dfrac{x+4}{4} = \dfrac{3x+1}{7}$.

A208. Solve for B in the equation $2F = \left(\dfrac{h}{3}\right)(2B + b)$.

A209. Given: $x - y + 9 = 0$ and $y = x^2 + 2x - 3$. Find their x and y intercepts of each.

A210. Given: $x - y + 9 = 0$ and $y = x^2 + 2x - 3$. Find where the two graphs intersect.

A211. The formula $t = \dfrac{\sqrt{d}}{4} + \dfrac{d}{1100}$ is used to calculate the number of seconds, t, it takes to hear a splash after dropping an object into a well that is d feet deep. Find the nearest hundredth of a second the number of seconds it takes to hear a splash after dropping an object into a well that is 200 feet deep.

A212. Gerry has decided to start a pebble collection. She collects one pebble the first day and two pebbles on the second day. On each subsequent day she collects one more pebble than the previous day. How many pebbles will Gerry have at the end of the twelfth day?

A213. Y varies directly as X. When Y = 18, X = 30. Find X when Y = 42.

A214. If $(x - 3)$ is a factor of $x^3 - 8x^2 + x + 42$, find the roots $x^3 - 8x^2 + x + 42 = 0$.

A215. Solve for the variable: $\dfrac{1}{x-1} - \dfrac{1}{x+1} = \dfrac{2}{x^2 - 1}$.

A216. Solve for x: $2|x + 8| - 6 = 0$

A217. Solve for the variable x: $5 + \dfrac{3x-7}{2} = \dfrac{2x-1}{3}$.

A218. Molly thinks of 3 integers. Adding them two at a time yields sums of 37, 41 and 44. What is the product of the three integers?

A219. Two people live 318 miles apart. They leave at the same time, and they drive towards each other until they meet and stop for lunch. The person driving east averages 57 mph which is 8 mph faster than the person driving west. How far does each person travel?

A220. A varies directly as B and indirectly as C. $A = \dfrac{2}{3}$ when $B = \dfrac{1}{4}$ and $C = \dfrac{3}{5}$. Find C when $A = \dfrac{3}{2}$ and $B = \dfrac{5}{6}$.

A221. Factor completely: $6x^3 + 25x^2 + 4x$.

A222. (-3, 3) and (3, 7) are points on a line. Find the equation of the line in the **y = mx + b** form.

A223. Simplify: $7 - 4\left(\dfrac{3^2 + 1}{7 - 3^2}\right) - (-2)^3$.

A224. Solve for x: $\dfrac{3}{1 + \dfrac{2}{3 - \frac{1}{3}}} = \dfrac{1}{x}$.

A225. Given f(x) = x + 9 and g(x) = x² + 2x – 3. For each function, find their x and y intercepts. Find the points that are common to both f(x) and g(x).

A226. Solve for C: $A = \dfrac{H}{2}(B + C)$.

A227. Two-thirds of a number minus one-sixth of a number is six more than three-eighths of the number. Find the number.

A228. Simplify: $\left(3a^2 - 2a + 3\right) \times (3a - 1)$.

A229. What number, when added to 1 and then divided by 7, has a result of 2?

A230. Solve for x: $2 + \dfrac{5}{1 + \dfrac{3}{2 - \dfrac{2}{5}}} = \dfrac{1}{x}$.

A231. Suppose that X and Y are integers. What is the remainder when $(5X + 13)(5Y + 3)$ is divided by 5?

A232. Running at an average rate of 6 meters per second, a sprinter ran to the end of the track and then jogged back to the starting point at an average rate of 2 meters per second. The total time for the sprint and jog back was 2 minutes 40 seconds. Find the length of the track.

A233. The numerator of a fraction is 23 more than the denominator. If the numerator is decreased by eight and the denominator is increased by 5, the resulting number is 2. What is the original fraction?

A234. (3, 3) and (-3, 7) are points on a line. Find the equation of the line.

A235. You are on a geo-cache hunt. Your GPS tells you that you are 40m away from the treasure. You walk 24m due west. The GPS compass now tells you that the treasure is due south from where you are standing. How far south do you need to go to find it?

N001. Simplify: $\dfrac{\dfrac{2}{3}+\dfrac{3}{4}}{1\dfrac{3}{5}-1\dfrac{1}{10}}$.

N002. Simplify: $\sqrt{841}-2\left[3-(7-11)\right]^2-4\left(3^2-2^3\right)^5$.

N003. If two different natural numbers have the same digits but in reverse order, each number is called the **palimage** of the other. For example, 368 and 863 are palimages of each other. What two different numbers between 40 and 60 are palimages of each other?

N004. What number multiplied by itself is equal to the product of 9 and 121

N005. Jess has \$5.10 worth of stamps. She has equal number of 50-cent, 20-cent, 10-cent, and 5-cent stamps. How many 50 cent stamps does she have?

N006. Tony has \$120 in his bank account. He deposits \$6 at the end of each week. Jenny has \$200 in her account, and she withdraws \$4 at the end of each week. After how many weeks will they each have the same amount in their accounts?

N007. Given the sequence: $\dfrac{7}{5}$, 2, $\dfrac{13}{5}$, $3\dfrac{1}{5}$, ... Find the seventh term.

N008. Consider $68 \bigcirc \dfrac{12}{5} = 70.4$. This statement is true if the symbol $\bigcirc$ is replaced by what particular arithmetic operation?

N009. What is the unit's digit of $7^{31}+3^{33}$.

N010. If \$90,000 is divided among Ann, Beth and Carol in the ratio of 8:7:3, respectively, what amount will Carol receive?

N011. The positive integer N is 100 less than one perfect square and 28 less than another perfect square. If N < 50, what is the value of N?

N012. Find three fractions between $\dfrac{2}{11}$ and $\dfrac{3}{11}$ that are equally spaced.

N013. For what integer x is 17(x + 3) a positive prime number?

N014. A rating number R_n can be assigned to any four-digit whole number in the following manner: R_n = (thousands' digit times 3) + hundreds' digit times 2) + (tens' digit times 1) + (ones' digit times 0). Find R_{7985} .

N015. A tornado usually travels at 25 to 40 mph. If you see a tornado approaching from half of a mile away, how much time does that give a person to take cover?

N016. A number pattern is described as follows: The first three terms are the first three perfect squares. Each term after the third term is the sum of the two preceding terms. What is the tenth term of this pattern?

N017. Change 1213_5 to a decimal number.

N018. In lowest terms, how much larger is $\dfrac{2003}{25} + 25$ than $\dfrac{2003 + 25}{25}$?

N019. Express the Roman Numeral **MMMCDXLVI** as a decimal number.

N020. Let 10101 − 1 be written as an integer in standard form. Find the sum of this integer's digits.

N021. When simplified, find the sum of the digits of $(10^{1996} - 1)$.

N022. Vin picks a number and multiples it by 3. He then adds 4 to the result and finally divides this new number by 2. His final result is 14. With what number did Vin start?

N023. Using a calculator, Joe divided the integer x into the integer y and the result was 1.0625. Both integers are less than 50 but Joe cannot remember what they were. What is the sum of all possible values of x and y?

N024. A semi prime number is defined as a number that is the product of two prime numbers. How many semi-prime numbers are less than 50?

N025. The year 2021 is a semi prime number. A semi prime number is a number that is the product of exactly two primes. Find the primes whose product is 2021.

N026. Raegan has three candles of the same length to provide light. Candle A burns for exactly 72 minutes. Candle B burns twice as fast as candle A. Candle C burns three times as fast as Candle B. What is the greatest total number of minutes of light that all three candles can provide?

N027. On a map, Tinsel Town and Emerald City measure $3\frac{1}{2}$ apart while the actual distance is 42 miles. If the distance between Emerald City and Tombstone measures $2\frac{3}{4}$ on the same map. How many actual miles apart are these two cities?

N028. A local movie theater is showing a 35 minute documentary on cyclones and a 42 minute documentary on tornados on two separate screens. If these documentaries both start a midnight, how many times during a 24 hour period will they start at the same time?

N029. Find the fraction in simplest form that is exactly halfway between $\frac{3}{7}$ and $\frac{4}{9}$.

N030. In a survey, 180 people were asked to select which form of exercise they preferred: running, swimming, or biking. Of the 180 people, 50% more people selected running over swimming. Five times as many people selected biking over swimming. How many people selected running as their favorite form of exercise?

N031. The arrangement $\boxed{a\ \ b\ \ c}$ means $(\,a \times b\,) \div c$. Express $\boxed{12\ \ 5\ \ 6}$ in simplest form .

N032. If D is the unit's digit of 6^{23} and E is the unit's digit of 2^{65}, find E^{D}.

N033. For how many values of Z is $\dfrac{60}{Z}$ also a whole number?

N034. Given the sequence: A, B, 7, C, D, E, F, G, H, I, J, 7, K, 4. If the sum of any three consecutive digits is 20, find the value of A.

N035. CD and DC each represent a two-digit number having the same digits, but in reverse order. If the difference of the two numbers is 54 and C + D = 10, find both CD and DC.

N036. Express $133_5 + 212_5 + 141_5$ as a base 5 numeral.

N037. The expression $\left(3^2 \right)^3 - 4$ is equal to a perfect square times a prime number. Find the prime number.

N038. Pauline has half as many dolls as Joyce. Joyce has half as many as Carrie. Carrie has 12 times Sophia. Sophia has 4 dolls. How many dolls do Carrie and Pauline have altogether?

N039. In the addition problem at the right, each letter represents a different digit. What digits do A, B, C, and D represent?

$$\begin{array}{r} 6\,B\,5\,2 \\ 9\,C\,4 \\ +\ A\,3\,7\,D \\ \hline 1\,1\,1\,1\,1 \end{array}$$

N040. The ratio of US citizens to noncitizens among patent applicants during a given period of time is 11:3. If 902 patent applicants were received from US citizens, how many were received from noncitizens?

N041. In his closet, Mike has 6 different T-shirts, 5 different pairs of shorts, and 2 different hats. Mike reaches into his closet and pulls out one T-shirt, one pair of shorts, and one hat. How many different combinations of one T-shirt, one pair of shorts and one hat are possible?

N042. Simplify: $\dfrac{\sqrt{2^6 + 2^6 + 2^6 + 4^3}}{\sqrt[3]{6 \times 15 \times 300}}$.

N043. A sport shop sold baseballs to teams in boxes of 8 and in boxes of 12. The inventory manager asked Moe, Curly and Larry for the baseball sold inventory during the past month. Moe reported that 8064 baseballs were sold; Curly reported that 8144 baseballs were sold; Larry reported that 8568 baseballs were sold. Which of the three employees reported the correct amount of baseballs sold?

N044. The Universal Set U = {1, 2, 3, . . . 17, 18}. Set A = {even integers less than 18}. Set B = {multiples of three less than 18}. Express $\overline{A} \cap \overline{B}$ as a list.

N045. Simplify: $2\sqrt{363} + 3\sqrt{180} - 3\sqrt{243}$.

N046. Find the smallest natural number that can be added to 259 so that the result is a multiple of 25.

N047. Six dozen equally priced oranges cost n dollars. In terms of n, what is the cost, in cents, of one orange.

N048. Six darts land on a dartboard. Each dart scores 2 or 5 or 8 points. Which of the follow total scores: 11, 16, 25, 36, 44, 51, is possible?

N049. Express: $\dfrac{2}{100} + \dfrac{3}{100} + \dfrac{4}{100} + \ldots + \dfrac{47}{100} + \dfrac{48}{100} + \dfrac{49}{100}$ as a simplified rational number.

N050. Find the 10th positive integer that is both odd and a multiple of 3.

N051. Find the greatest common factor and least common multiple of 774 and 2484.

N052. Colored beads are placed in the following order: 1 blue, 1 yellow; then 2 blue, 2 yellow; then 3 blue, 3 yellow; and so on. In all, how many of the first 100 beads are blue?

N053. One owl hoots every 3 hours. Another owl hoots every 8 hours. A third owl hoots every 12 hours. At one time the three owls hoot together. In the next 80 hours, how many times do the three owls hoot at the same.

N054. Marilyn Monroe was born in an interesting year. The tens digit was twice the thousands digit, the ones digit was three times the tens digit, and the hundreds digit was equal to the sum of the other three digits. In what year was Marilyn born?

N055. For every two doowops that are bought at the regular price, a third doowop can be bought for $4. Nine doowops were bought for a total of $90. Find the price of a doowop sold at the regular price.

N056. Express 11001101_2 as a decimal number.

N057. If a $= 2^8 3^4 19^2 7$ and b $= 2^5 3^2 19$, find $\dfrac{9b}{a}$.

N058. How many different natural numbers less than 200 are exactly divisible by either 6 or 9 or by both?

N059. Each term of a sequence is one more than twice the term before it. If the first term is 1, what is the sum of the first five terms?

N060. In an arithmetic sequence, the 7th term is 30 and the 11th term is 60. What is the 21st term?

N061. Two watches are set correctly at 7 AM. One watch gains 3 minutes every two hours. The other watch loses 1 minute every two hours. What is the correct time (AM or PM) the next day when the faster watch be exactly one hour ahead of the slower watch?

N062. There are exactly 10 disks in a bowl and each is marked with a different natural number from 1 to 10. Gino and Fran each select 5 disks. Two of Gino's disks are marked 2 and 8. Two of Fran's disks are marked 7 and 9. What is the largest sum that Gino can have?

N063. The addition problem at the right yields a sum of CD6E. A, B, C, D, and E are all different digits. What 4 digit number does CD6E represent?

```
  A A A
+   B B
-------
C D 6 E
```

N064. What is the largest prime factor of $3^6 + 2^8$?

N065. Each year Alex gets a raise of 8% plus an additional $100. In 2018, Alex's annual salary was $47,563.84. What will Alex's salary (correct to nearest cent) be in 2020?

N066. Marcie bought 120 apples for $24. When she got home, she discovered that one-fifth of the apples were rotten. If she figured she spent the $24 on only good apples, how much did each good apple actually cost?

N067. You find yourself at the bottom of an ice cave that is 50 feet deep. You are able to climb up 10 feet each day but you slip down 2 feet at night. How many days will it take you to reach the top and escape the cave?

N068. How many different 3 digit numbers can be made using only the digits 2, 5, and 9?

N069. A set of eleven consecutive even whole numbers has a sum of 374. What is the sum of the first and last even whole number in this set?

N070. Numbers such as 763 and 652 have their digits in _decreasing order_ because each digit is less than the digit to its left. The digit 655 is _not_ in decreasing order. How many whole numbers between 100 and 599 have their digits in decreasing order?

N071. Considering the number 507,400, the last two zeroes are called terminal zeroes. The zero between 5 and 7 is not considered a terminal zero. How many terminal zeroes are there in 30!

N072. What is the unit's digit of $2^{93} + 3^{91}$?

N073. The 3rd, 4th, and 5th floors of a building are being remodeled and the rooms renumbered using all the whole numbers from 300 to 599. How many numerals for the digit 3 will be needed to number these rooms?

N074. One light flashes every 2 minutes and another light flashes every 7 minutes. If both lights flash together at 1 PM, what is the first time after 3 PM that both lights flash together?

N075. In a set of natural numbers, all have different values. The sum of this set of numbers is 350. The average of this set of numbers is 50. One of the numbers is 100. What is the largest number that can be in this set?

N076. Given the sequence: $\dfrac{1}{3}, \dfrac{7}{6}, 2, \dfrac{17}{6}$, find the 87th term.

N077. Find the natural numbers that each leave a remainder of 2 when divided into 83.

N078. The numbers 10, A, 16, B, C, 25 are in order. The difference between 10 and A, A and 16, 16 and B, B and C, and C and 25 are all the same. Find the number that C represents.

N079. Find the GCF and LCM of 1428, 1785, 2499.

N080. Kyle's birthday party in 2020 cost d dollars per person and p people attended. In 2021, the cost per person doubled and the number of people attending also doubled. What is the ratio of the total cost of the party in 2020 to the total cost of the party in 2021?

N081. Find 2.5% of 2.5% expressed as a percent.

N082. If D is the unit's digit of 17^{23} and E is the unit's digit of 13^{26}. Which is greater D^E or E^D.

N083. The first odd positive number is 1. The sum of the first two odd positive numbers is 4. What is the sum of the first 25 odd positive numbers?

N084. The numerator of a fraction (not necessarily in lowest terms) is 7 less than the denominator. If the fraction is subtracted from 1, the result is $\dfrac{1}{3}$. Find the fraction.

N085. How many 3 digit even numbers are there that have 24 as the sum of their digits? Name them.

N086. Simplify: $\dfrac{1}{100} + \dfrac{2}{100} + \dfrac{3}{100} + \ldots + \dfrac{996}{100} + \dfrac{997}{100} + \dfrac{998}{100}$ and express the answer as a decimal.

N087. If (a)(b) = 10, (b)(c) = 12, (a)(c) = 30, express the value of (a)(b)(c) in simplest form.

N088. Simplify: $\left[2\left(n^2\right)^{-2}\right]^2$ and express the answer with positive exponents.

N089. What are the last two digits of: 7^{2014} .

N090. A **fast** clock gains time at the same rate every hour. It is set to the correct time at 10 AM. When the **fast** clock shows 11 AM the same day, the correct time is 10:52 AM. What is the correct time when the **fast** clock shows 3:30 PM the same day?

N091. Joey has 17 coins with a value of 76¢. The coins are pennies, nickels, and dimes. He has twice as many pennies as dimes. How many nickels does Joey have?

N092. If F is the unit's digit of 2^{49} and G is the unit's digit of 7^{49}, find F + G.

N093. Given $f(x) = \sqrt{\sqrt{x} - 1}$ for all x, x ≥ 1. Find $f(100)$.

N094. A fraction $\dfrac{a}{b}$ (not necessarily in lowest terms) is equal to $\dfrac{5}{9}$. When 5 is added to the denominator of $\dfrac{a}{b}$, the value of the new fraction is $\dfrac{1}{2}$. Find a + b .

N095. Jillian has a total of \$82 consisting of an equal number of pennies, nickels, dimes, and quarters. How many coins does she have in all?

N096. Customers at a participating yogurt shop may select one of three flavors of yogurts. They may choose one of four toppings. How many one-flavor, one-topping combinations are possible?

N097. Lanna has \$4.05 in dimes and quarters. If she has 5 more quarters than dimes, how many dimes does Lanna have?

N098. In an election for a seat on the finance committee, Ted receives $\dfrac{5}{9}$ of the votes. Gary receives $\dfrac{2}{11}$ of the votes and Frank receives the remainder of the votes. Express Frank's total votes as a fraction.

N099. If D = 1 + 3 + 5 + . . . + 95 + 97 + 99 and E = 2 + 4 + 6 + . . . + 94 + 96 + 98, which is greater D or E, and by how much?

N100. Simplify: $\sqrt{\dfrac{13}{56}} \times \sqrt{\dfrac{7}{26}}$.

N101. In one complete day at flower stand, a man can arrange 100 bouquets of flowers and his helper can arrange one-quarter as many bouquets. If they take turns working complete days, how many days would it take them to arrange 500 bouquets of flowers?

N102. A jewelry artisan is making earring hoops. Each hoop requires a piece of wire $3\dfrac{3}{4}$ inches long. If the wire comes in a 50 inch coil, how many earrings can be made? How much wire, if any, is wasted?

N103. The Hookum Corporation common stock now sells for $10\dfrac{1}{2}$, which represents a reduction of $12\dfrac{1}{2}\%$ over last year's average price. Find last year's average price.

N104. Brian has earned 60 markers he could turn in at the end of the semester for extra-credit points. Some markers are worth one point and others are worth two points. If he has a total of 83 extra credit points, how many one-point markers does he have?

N105. Find the largest factor of 2520 that is not divisible by 6.

N106. On a scale drawing, item A is 5 inches in length and item B is 11 inches in length. If the actual size of item B is 5 meters, find the actual size of A expressed as an exact value.

N107. A candy store is having a special on certain wrapped candy selling for 3¢ and 8¢. What is the largest amount a buyer can spend that cannot be made with the 3¢ and 8¢ candy?

N108. Consider all pairs of natural numbers whose sum is less than 11. The two members of a pair could be either the same as each other or different. How many different products are possible if the two numbers are multiplied?

N109. All natural numbers are arranged in the triangular pattern as shown by the first four rows at the right. What is the first number in the 13th row?

$$
\begin{array}{c}
1 \\
2 \quad 3 \quad 4 \\
5 \quad 6 \quad 7 \quad 8 \quad 9 \\
10 \quad 11 \quad 12 \quad 13 \quad 14 \quad 15 \quad 16
\end{array}
$$

N110. On a map, one-third of an inch represents 5 miles. On a map, if NYC and Portland, Maine are 18 inches apart, what is the actual distance between the two cities?

N111. A movie theatre is having a 24 hour Three Stooges movies marathon with "Disorder in the Court", "Wee Wee Monsiour" and "An Ache in Every Stake" as the featured films. The films are 105 minutes, 84 minutes and 60 minutes long respectively. If all three movie start at midnight, how many times will they begin at the same time during this 24 hour time period?

N112. One case holds 2 cartons. Each carton holds 3 boxes. Each box holds 4 bundles. Each bundle holds 5 envelopes. Each envelope holds 6 pencils. What is the largest number of pencils that one case can hold?

N113. White Rain shampoo offers two sizes: Regular is priced at $2.88 for a 12 ounce bottle and Family priced at $5.07 for 22 ounces. Which size is the best value?

N114. Express as a simplified common fraction: $\dfrac{2 + 4 + 6 + \ldots + 1338 + 1340 + 1342}{3 + 6 + 9 + \ldots + 2007 + 2010 + 2013}$.

N115. Farmer Hank has less than 100 pigs on his farm. If he groups the pigs five per pen, there is always 3 pigs left over. If he groups the pigs seven to a pen, there is always 1 pig left over. If he groups the pigs three to a pen, there are no pigs left over. What is the greatest number of pigs Farmer Hank can have on his farm?

N116. The Rhombus Nail Salon must pay $5,000 for rent each month at its Newbury Street location. In addition, their monthly electricity bill is $1.45 per kilowatt of electricity used. If the total cost of both rent and electricity in January was $16,520.45, how many kilowatt hours of electricity was used by the nail salon?

N117. Find the least of 3 consecutive integers whose product is 10626.

N118. In the sequence x, y, 23, 43, 83, ... each term after the first term, x, is formed by doubling the previous term and then subtracting 3. What is the value of x + y?

N119. Sarah and Michael each start with the same number of cents. Sarah buys one candy bar and has 70¢ left. Michael buys three candy bars at the same price and has 20¢ left. How many cents did Sarah start with?

N120. In 2010 the price of a certain antique car was 30% greater than in 2005. In 2015 the price of the same car was 50% greater than in 2010. The price of the car was what percent greater in 2015 than in 2005?

N121. Find the whole number which is: (1) less than 100; (2) a multiple of 3; (3) a multiple of 5; (4) odd; (5) the sum of the digits is odd.

N122. Given the sequence: $\dfrac{2}{7}, \dfrac{1}{2}, \dfrac{7}{8}$, find the seventh term and express it as the ratio of two integers.

N123. Find the sum of the digits of $10^{50} - 1$.

N124. A factory has enough oil on hand to last 30 days if 4 barrels of oil are used each day. How many barrels should be used per day if the same amount of oil is to last 40 days?

N125. If x and y are positive integers such that $x^y = 8$, what is the maximum possible value of x + y?

N126. If $3^2 + 4^2 + 5^2 + 6^2 = a^2 + b^2$, find a + b.

N127. A 14-digit number N is created by writing 8 as both the first and last digit and then placing the 3-digit number 793 between the two 8s four times. What is the remainder when N is divided by 7?

N128. N = 8A65B in which A and B are digits and N is divisible by 24. What is the smallest number that N can be?

N129. If $S = 1 - \dfrac{1}{3} + \dfrac{1}{5} - \dfrac{1}{7} + \dfrac{1}{9} - \dfrac{1}{11}$ and $T = 1 - \dfrac{1}{3} + \dfrac{1}{5} - \dfrac{1}{7}$, expressed as a fraction, S is how much greater than T?

N130. Joe Zizza bakes 90 pizzas. Each pizza is cut either into 8 small slices or 6 large slices. Joe has 5 small slices for every 3 large slices. How many of the 90 pizzas are cut into small slices?

N131. What is the largest possible sum that can result from **BAD + CAD + DAC** if each letter represents a different digit, chosen from: 1, 3, 8, and 9?

N132. Given universal set U = {positive even numbers less than 30}. A = {8, 12, 16, 20, 24, 28}, B = {2, 8, 14, 20}, and C = {14, 20, 26}. Find $A \cap C$ and $(A \cap B) \cup C$

N133. Find the 4 digit number ABCD, if ABCD when multiplied by 9 results in DCBA.

N134. If a is $\dfrac{2}{3}$ of b and b is $\dfrac{1}{4}$ of c, what fraction of c is a?

N135. Find my number: (1) This number is 1 less than a prime number. (2) It is greater than 5 but less than 45. (3) The sum of its digits is a prime number. (4) It is the largest number that satisfies all of the above.

N136. If $\dfrac{1}{6}$ is written as a decimal to 200 places, what is the sum of the first 100 digits to the right of the decimal point?

N137. Each of 8 boxes contains at least one marble. Each box contains a different number of marbles, except for two boxes which contain the same number of marbles. What is the smallest total number of marbles that the 8 boxes contain?

N138. If $\dfrac{1}{3}$ of $1\dfrac{1}{3}$ is added to $\dfrac{1}{6}$ of $1\dfrac{1}{6}$, express this sum as a fraction in simplest form.

N139. Gino has 8 marbles. Each marble weighs either 2 g, 4 g, or 5 g. He has a different number of marbles with at least one of each weight. What is the smallest possible total weight of Gino's marbles?

N140. Joyce throws five darts at the target
Shown at the right. Each dart lands
In a region of the target, scoring the
Points shown below. Of the following
Total scores, list all that are **not** possible.
6, 14, 17, 38, 42, 58

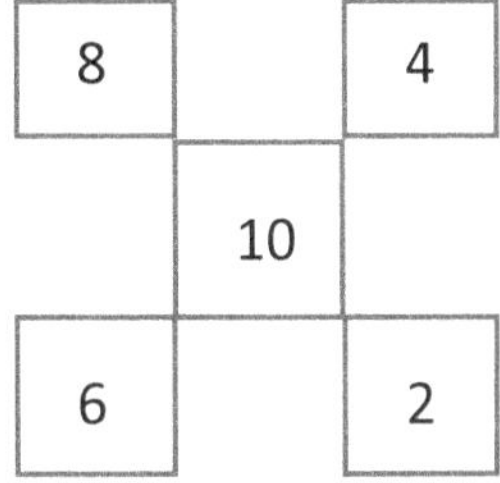

N141. Mac's Ice Cream sells 25 double scoop ice cream cones. 12 contain at least one scoop of vanilla, 8 contain at least one scoop of chocolate and 6 contain a scoop of each. How many cones contain neither a scoop of vanilla nor a scoop of chocolate?

N142. An odd number between 301 and 370 has three different digits. If the sum of the digits is five times the hundreds digit, find the number.

N143. Find the missing number A in the sequence: 2, 6, 12, 20, A, 42, 56.

N144. If A is the unit's digit of 7^{35} and B is the unit's digit of 4^{35}, what is the product of A and B?

N145. Given: $f(x) = x^2 - 3,\ g(x) = 2x - 7,\ h(x) = \dfrac{2x - 1}{x + 1}$. Find $f\left(\dfrac{1}{4}\right)$ and $g\left(h\left(\dfrac{5}{3}\right)\right)$.

N146. The numbers 1, 2, 3, and 4 are
placed in the empty squares so
that each row, each column, and
each diagonal contains each of the
four numbers. Find the value of **A**
and the value of **B**.

[A = 2, B = 1]

1	2	3	4
4			1
A	B		

N147. in a 60 inch coil of wire, how many earrings can be made if each earring requires $3\frac{2}{3}$ inches of wire? How much wire, if any is wasted?

N148. A regular 8 by 8 checkerboard has 32 black and 32 red squares. John colors one-half the red squares black. Then Jane colors one-fourth of all the black squares red. How many red squares are on the checkerboard now?

N149. If a Ω b = 3a − 4b, find 5 Ω (2 Ω 3).

N150. Kari spends one-third of her lottery winnings on outstanding college loans, one-fifth of it on entertainment, 30% of it on clothes and the remaining \$16,500 is invested on a high risk, high yield stock. How much were her lottery winnings?

N151. Tito collects stamps. Each day he adds 4 stamps to his collection. At the end of three days, he has 50 stamps. How many stamps does Tito have at the end of 10 days?

N152. In the subtraction problem at the right, **AB5C** and
47D6 represent 4-digit numbers. What number
Does AB5C represent?

$$\begin{array}{r} AB5C \\ -\ 47D6 \\ \hline 1998 \end{array}$$

N153. What is the smallest positive number that has a remainder of 1 when divided by 4, a remainder of 2 when divided by 5, and a remainder of 3 when divided by 6?

N154. Simplify: $999{,}999{,}999{,}999^2 - 999{,}999{,}999{,}998^2$.

N155. Dan and Nick work at a factory. Dan can complete 250 units of work in one week while Nick can complete 175 units of work during the same week. In how many weeks will Dan have completed 975 more units of work than Nick?

N156. If $a + b + c + d = 982$ and $b + d = 985$, what is the value of $a - b + c - d$?

N157. Simplify: $\dfrac{399}{\dfrac{1}{1 + \dfrac{1}{2}} + \dfrac{2}{2 + \dfrac{2}{3}} + \dfrac{3}{3 + \dfrac{3}{4}}}$.

N158. Express the fraction $\dfrac{7}{9}$ as an exact value percent.

N159. Dottie gets 70% on a 10-problem test, 80% on a 20-problem test and 90% on a 30-problem test. If the three tests are combined into a 60-problem test, what fraction of this new test did she get correct?

N160. At 7 AM a volume of gas has 500 bacteria particles in it. At 11 AM after a filtering treatment, the same volume of gas has 300 bacteria particles remaining. What is the percent of decrease of the bacteria particles?

N161. Find a two digit number with all of the following properties: the first digit is larger than the second digit, the difference between the digits is great than 3, the sum of the digits is greater than 10, and the number is a multiple of 12.

N162. The distance from Earth to the Moon is approximately 2.4×10^5 miles. A satellite crosses the path between Earth and the Moon at a distance of 240 miles from Earth. What fraction of the distance from Earth to the Moon is the satellite's distance from Earth at this point? Express the answer as common fraction with numerator and denominator in integer form

N163. How many 2-digit numbers have digits whose sum is a perfect square?

N164. One morning Christine took out half of the coins from her coin bank, and in the evening, she put in 20 coins. The next morning, she took out one third of the coins in the bank, and that evening she put in 4 coins. The next morning, she took out half the coins in the bank, leaving 15 coins. How many coins were in the bank to begin with?

N165. What percent of the first 1 million positive integers are perfect squares?

N166. Ten people stand in line. The first goes to the back of the line and the next person sits down, so that the person who was third is now first in line. Now that person goes to the back of the line and the next person sits down. The process is repeated until only one person remains. What was the original position in line of the only remaining person?

N167. For what value of k is the ratio of $\sqrt{2002}$ to $\sqrt{2002k}$ the same as the ratio of $\sqrt{5}$ to $\sqrt{2}$?

N168. Barbara delivered newspapers to each house on her side of the street. The houses on her side of the street begin with number 599 and each increase by 6. The last house number was the largest possible not over 799. How many papers did Barbara deliver each day?

N169. If $8^r = 32^{12}$, what whole number is equal to $4^r \div 8^{10}$.

N170. While practicing for the Yarmouth Local Olympics, Harold swam 5 miles in one hour, rode a bike 100 miles averaging 25 miles per hour and then ran 15 miles averaging 5 miles per hour. What was Harold's average rate of speed for the entire practice session?

N171. Arrange the digits 1, 1, 2, 2, 3, 3, as a six-digit number in which the 1's are separated by one digit, the 2's are separated by two digits, and the 3's are separated by three digits.

N172. Find the first five common multiples of 45 and 35.

N173. On June 1st, the swimming pool at Foster Park held 150,000 gallons of water. On sunny days 500 gallons of water evaporate. On cloudy days 200 gallons of water evaporate. On partly cloudy days 300 gallons of water evaporate. One-third of the days in June were cloudy, two-fifths were partly cloudy and the rest were sunny. How many gallons of water must be added on July 1st to fill the pool back to its original amount?

N174. Find all common factors of 88 and 108.

N175. The odometer on Mr. Verdugo's car shows that he has traveled 62,222 miles. What is the least number of miles that Mr. Verdugo must travel before the odometer again shows 4 of the 5 digits the same as each other?

N176. In 2019 there were 2112 foreclosures in the state of Ohio. In 2020, there were 6324 foreclosures in the state of Ohio. What is the percent of increase (to the nearest whole number) in foreclosures for Ohio during this time interval?

N177. If $\left(4^5\right)\left(5^{13}\right)$ is written as an integer, how many digits are in this integer?

N178. How many numbers are there that have the sum of their digits equal to 100 and the product of their digits equal to 5?

N179. Simplify: $7 - 4\left(\dfrac{3^2 + 1}{7 - 3^2}\right) - (-2)^2$.

N180. At a "society" breakfast, one-half of the people had 3 cups of coffee. One-third of the people had 2 cups of coffee and the remaining 8 people had only one cup of coffee. How many cups of coffee were served at the "society" breakfast?

N181. Your annual salary as a starting teacher is $50,000. The school district is having financial difficulty but in an effort to not cut teachers, offers you a deal of a 5% reduction in salary with the promise to increase your salary the year after the reduction to $54,000. What percent increase (to the nearest tenth) is needed to get to the promised amount?

N182. In a certain class, there are twice as many girls as boys. One-half of the boys and two-thirds of the girls are studying physics. What fraction of the entire class is studying physics?

N183. Find all d in the numeral 68349577235843d6 so that it is divisible by 4.

N184. A recursive sequence of numbers is defined as follows: $a_1 = 10$, $a_2 = 15$, $a_n = (a_{n-1} - a_{n-2})^2$ for $n > 2$. What is the value of a_5?

N185. Given 10, 27, 53, 97, 168, ... Find the next term.

N186. Exactly one of the numbers 2, 3, 5, and 7 is placed in each of the 4 regions formed by circles A, B, C. The sum of the numbers in each circle is the same? What is that sum?

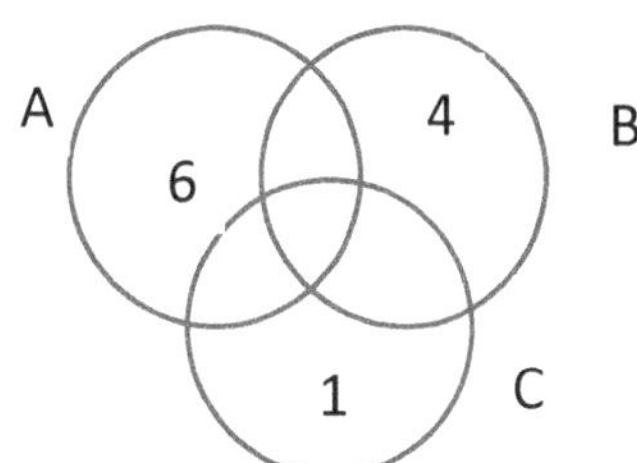

N187. Find all d in the numeral 68349577235843d6 so that it is divisible by 6.

N188. There are 72 boys and 90 girls present for an elementary school math competition. Mr. Foley would like to arrange all of the students in equal rows with only girls and boys in each row. What is the greatest number of students that can be in each row?

N189. Joe's pay after 7% was deducted for social security tax and 15% was deducted for federal income tax was $117. What was Joe's pay before the deductions?

N190. Tim baked at least two dozen cookies but fewer than 60 cookies. If he divides the cookies evenly among 7 plates, 4 cookies are left over. If he divides the cookies evenly among 6 plates, 5 cookies are left over. How many cookies did Tim bake?

N191. If $m \triangle n = 2m + n$ and $m \nabla n = 4m - n$, find $2 \triangle (5 \nabla 3)$.

N192. Solve for x: $\left(\dfrac{2^{-3}}{3^{-2}} \right)\left(\dfrac{x^{-1}}{2^{-3} + 3^{-2}} \right) = \dfrac{1}{3}$.

N193. If $P = (2 - 3 - 4 + t)^{2347}$ and $Q = (-2 + 3 + 4 - 7)^{2347}$. Find $(2 + 3 + 4 + 7)^{P + Q}$.

N194. List the natural numbers less than 50 that have exactly three factors.

N195. Simplify: $\left(\dfrac{4^{-1} + 5^{-1}}{2^{-3} + 3^{-2}} \right)\left(\dfrac{6^{-2}}{3^{-3}} \right)$

N196. Simplify and express answer with positive exponents: $\dfrac{\left(a^{-3}b^2 \right)^{-4}}{\left(a^{-5}b^2 \right)^3}$.

N197. The digits 1, 2, 3, 4, and 5 are each used to create a five-digit number ABCDE. The three digit number ABC is divisible by 4, BCD is divisible by 5, and CDE is divisible by 3. Find the five-digit number ABCDE.

N198. Express the given repeating decimal $0.5\overline{3}$ as a fraction in simplest form.

N199. A fuel company charges monthly finance fees of 1.2% for the first $500 and 0.8% for any amount over $500. What is the monthly finance fee for an account with a balance of $950?

N200. Find the sum of the first 200 multiples of 5.

N201. How many digits are in the standard numeral for 2^{33} X 5^{28} ?

N202. Find the sum of the odd numbers that are factors of 240.

N203. Carol makes 10 cups of punch by using three times as much lemonade as grape juice. Julie drinks one cup of this punch then realizes that Carol needs 10 cups of punch. Julie tries to help by adding one cup of grape juice to the pitcher of punch. What is the ratio of lemonade to grape juice in this new pitcher of punch?

N204. Given $g(x) = \dfrac{3x - 7}{6 - 5x^2}$. Find $g(a + 1)$.

N205. If f(x) = 7x + b and g(x) = 3x + d and f(g(x)) = g(f(x)). Determine the value of $\dfrac{b}{d}$.

N206. Simplify: $\dfrac{2^{-3}}{5^{-1}}\left(\dfrac{3^{-2}+3}{6^{-1}+8^{-1}} \right)$.

N207. Using pennies, nickels and dimes, how many different ways can you make 25 cents?

N208. Sarah swims laps at a pool. When she first started, she swam 10 laps in 25 minutes. Now she swims 12 laps in 24 minutes. By how minutes has Sarah improved her lap time?

N209. What is the unit's digit of $7^{31} + 3^{33}$.

N210. One seat in an auditorium is broken. It is in the 3rd row from the front of the auditorium and in the 18th row from the back of the auditorium. There are 12 seats to the left of the broken seat and 17 seats to its right. If every row has the same number of seats, how many unbroken seats are in this auditorium?

N211. A new mathematical symbol (¶) was created. A ¶ B is equal to 3 less than the sum of the product of A and B and the square of B. Find the value of 11 ¶ 7 .

N212. In a certain storage shed, there are fewer than 92 crates. If the crates are stacked 6 to a stack, 4 crates remain. If the crates are stacked 5 to a stack, 3 remain. How many crates are in the storage shed?

N213. Change $42\dfrac{6}{7}\%$ to a fraction in simplest form.

N214. The GCF of a pair of numbers is 18 and the LCM is 180. If one number is 90, what is the other?

N215. What is the greatest number of Mondays that can occur in 45 consecutive days?

N216. Find the GCF and LCM of 2904 and 5148 .

N217. Find the whole number value of n: $\dfrac{3}{80}<\dfrac{1}{n}<\dfrac{4}{101}$.

N218. The prime factorization of the whole number M can be written: $M=p^{3}t$ where p and t are distinct prime numbers. Find all the factors of M.

N219. Let X equal 157 plus its palimage. Let Y equal the sum of X and its palimage. Let Z equal the sum of Y and its palimage. What is Z?

N220. Find all common factors of 84 and 112.

N221. Find D so that 2143453672819D72 is divisible by 11.

N222. The binary number 101101 is equal to what decimal number.

N223. The ratio of two positive integers is 5:2. Their product is 160. Find both integers.

N224. $a\,\Omega\,b=3a-4b$. Find $5\,\Omega\,(\,2\,\Omega\,3)$.

N225. The first term of an arithmetic sequence is −37. The second term is −30. What is the smallest positive term of this sequence?

N226. Express $0.1\overline{72}$ as a fraction in simplest form.

N227. Cassie can bake at most 90 cookies at one time. If she divides the cookies evenly among 6 plates, 3 cookies are left over. If she then divides the cookies evenly among 7 plates, 3 cookies are left over. Given her plating options, what is the largest amount of cookies that Cassie can bake?

N228. Find the sum of the 15th and 19th terms of the sequence of numbers: 1, 3, 6, 10, 15, ...

N229. If $\dfrac{5}{6}$ is written as a decimal to 100 places, what is the sum of the first 100 digits to the right of the decimal point?

N230. How many pairs of numbers between 30 and 100 are palimages of each other?

N231. To engrave a word on a metal plate, each of the first three letters cost 5¢, and each letter after the first three costs 1¢ more than the preceding letter does. Find the cost of engraving the word: **MATHEMATICS**.

N232. The ratio of girls to boys in Miss Quinn's class of 25 students is 3:2. The ratio of girls to boys in Miss Brown's class of 27 students is 2:1. What is the total number of girls in both classes?

N233. Jess wrote a list of 2000 consecutive odd positive integers. By how much would the largest integer on her list exceed the smallest integer on her list?

N234. There are red, white, and blue marbles in a bag in the ratio of 2:3:4. The bag contains 108 marbles. How many of each color are in the bag?

N235. Let $D = \dfrac{A^2 B^4}{C^3}$. R equals the value of the expression that results when the positive numbers A and B are doubled, and C is tripled in the expression for D. Then R is how many times D?

N236. What is the smallest natural number that is a multiple of each even number from 10 to 20 inclusive?

N237. You are buying cups, plates, and napkins for a school function. Cups come in packs of 24, plates come in packs of 30, and napkins come in packs of 100. What is the least number of packs of napkins that you need to buy if you want to buy the exact same number of cups, plates, and napkins?

N238. The odd numbers from 1 to 17
are placed in the magic square
at the right so that the sum of the
numbers in each row, column, and
diagonal are equal. What number
goes in the square marked **X** ?

	1	
5		X
7		3

N239. In the number 12345, the value represented by the digit 4 is what fraction of the value represented by the digit 2?

N240. Three Math Team students practice at different times: 9:00 AM, 11 AM, and 1 PM. Jack practices either at 11 AM or at 1 PM. Kellie doesn't practice at 11 AM, Linda doesn't practice at 1 PM, and Kellie practices 2 hours before Linda. At what time does each student practice?

N241. The pages of a book are numbered consecutively, beginning with 1. The digit 7 is printed 25 times in numbering the pages. What is the largest number of pages the book can have?

N242. If $3 \times \theta - 25 = 8$, then the value of $3 \times \theta + 25$.

N243. Find the sum of all positive integers less than 100 that are divisible by 3 but not divisible by 2 .

N244. Find d in the numeral 68349577235843d6 so that it is divisible by 4 .

N245. Find d in the numeral 68349577235843d6 so that it is divisible by 6 .

N246. The sum of three numbers is 136. The ratio of the first to the second is 2:3. The ratio of the second to the third is 6:7. Find the three numbers.

N247. Taylor claims that she can beat anyone in her class in the 400 yard run by 15 seconds. So far, the fastest time has been 2 minutes, 4 seconds. In order to live up to her claim, what time must Taylor record in the 400 yard run?

N248. Solve this Elusive Equation. Write out the digits, left to right, 1 through 9. Insert 2 addition signs and 2 subtraction signs to make a mathematical expression that is equal to 100.

N249. A number has 5 different digits, none of which are zero. The first digit plus the second digit equals the third digit. Twice the third digit plus the second digit equals the fifth digit. The first digit equals twice the second digit. Four times the first digit equals the fourth digit. The fourth digit minus the second digit equals the fifth digit. Find the number.

N250. Find d in the numeral 68349577235843d6 so that it is divisible by 8.

N251. How many positive integers less than 100 can be written as the product of the first two powers of two different prime numbers?

N252. Find d in the numeral 68349577235843d6 so that it is divisible by 9.

N253. A square picture $2\frac{1}{2}$ feet wide is to be hung on a wall so that the center of the picture is 4 feet from the ceiling. How far is the top of the picture from the ceiling?

N254. A number like 123 or 479 is called a "rising number". A "rising number" is such that each digit in the number is greater than the digit to its immediate left. Find the number of 3-digit "rising number".

N255. A digital clock shows time in the form HH: MM. On a certain day, what is the number of minutes between 7:59 AM and 2: 59 PM that HH is greater than MM?

N256. Ryan, a Pop Warner football player weighs 65 pounds but in his football uniform he weighs72 pounds. His father is a semi-pro football player for the Hyde Park Stampeders and weighs 260 pounds. How much would Ryan's father uniform weigh if the ratio of uniform weight to body weight is the same for Ryan and his father?

N257. Find d in the numeral 68349577235843d6 so that it is divisible by 11.

N258. What is the sum of the integers between 1 and 300 that are divisible by 11 or 13 or both.

N259. What whole number between 100 and 200 is both a perfect square and a multiple of 7?

N260. What is the remainder when 579346212247897 is divided by: (1) 3, (2) 9,   (3) 11 ?

N261. In an election Ted receives $\dfrac{4}{9}$ of the votes. Gary receives $\dfrac{3}{11}$ of the vote and Frank receives the remainder of the votes. Express Frank's total as a fraction. Rank the candidates from top to bottom by the fraction of the votes they obtained.

N262. Simplify: $\left(\sqrt{4! \cdot 3!} \right)^2$.

N263. If $(x)(y) = 8$ and $(y)(z) = 16$ and $(x)(z) = 50,$ express the value of $(x)(y)(z)$ in simplest form.

N264. Justin wrote the integers from 1 to 104 inclusive. How many digits did Justin write?

N265. Solve for x: $x^{-1}\left(\dfrac{3^{-1}}{2^{-2}+3^{-2}} \right) = \dfrac{3}{4}$.

N266. Using the following definition of ø : A ø B means $B - 2A + 3$. Find the value of 2 ø 6. Find all values of x such that x ø 9 = 0 .

N267. Simplify: $\left(\dfrac{6^{-1}}{2^{-3}} \right)\left(\dfrac{4^{-1}-3^{-2}}{8^{-1}+3^{-2}} \right)$.

N268. What is the ratio of 8 feet to 28 inches?

N269. If$(a)(b) = 168,$ $(b)(c) = 54,$ $(a)(c) = 63,$ express the value of $(a)(b)(c)$ in simplest form.

N270. Kate rode her bike for 30 minutes at 16 mph, then walked for 90 minutes at a speed of 4 mph. What was Kate's overall average speed.

N271. What is the unit's digit of $2^{61} + 4^{38}$.

N272. Simplify: $6^{-1} + 4^{-1} - 2^{-1}$.

N273. Find the different integers a, b, c, and d that satisfy: $1729 = a^3 + b^3 = c^3 + d^3$.

N274. Ron's PIN number written as a four binary numbers is: 0101–1000–0011–1001. What is Ron's four digit PIN number written as a decimal number?

N275. When the six-digit number 3456N7 is divided by 8, the remainder is 5. Find all possible values of the digit N.

N276. If x is three less than $\dfrac{n}{2}$, find an expression for n in terms of x.

N277. John has 4-foot poles and 6-foot poles. If he lays all the 4-ft poles in a line, they have the same total length as laying all the 6-ft poles in a line. Altogether he has 20 poles. How many 6 foot poles does John have?

N278. A movie theater seats 100 and is full for a Saturday movie. Adult seats sell for $9 each and seats for children sell for $5 each. If the theater collects $640 in ticket sales for the movie, how many seats for children were sold?

N279. Find all values of d so that 27296958573d5 is divisible by 11.

N280. The sum of three numbers is 112. The ratio of the first to the second is 2:3. The ratio of the second to the third is 9:13. Find the three numbers?

N281. The product of two consecutive odd integers is 675. Find the integers.

N282. Complete the following: $235_{(8)} = \underline{\hspace{1cm}}_{(5)} = \underline{\hspace{1cm}}_{(12)} = \underline{\hspace{1cm}}_{(2)}$

N283. Express $n = 0.4\overline{35}$ as a rational number in simplest form.

N284. Liz was given an ant farm by her grandparents for her 20th birthday. The farm could hold a total of 100,000 ants. Liz's farm had 1,500 ants when it was given to her. If the number of ants in the farm on the day after her birthday was 3,000 and the number of ants the day after that was 6,000, in how many days will the farm be full?

N285. Given 78453393261366F. Find F so that the number is divisible by 6.

N286. If u is the unit's digit of 3^{33} and v is the unit's digit of 2^{38}. Find $3^{-2}(u^v)^2 - 2^{-3}(v^u)^2$

N287. Given 78453393261366F. Find F so that the number is divisible by 11.

N288. Simplify: $\dfrac{7^{-2}}{5^{-1}}\left(\dfrac{56^{-1}+7^{-1}}{2^{-2}+3^{-1}}\right)$

N289. Angela picks a number and multiplies it by 3. She then adds 4 to the result and finally divides this new number by 2. Her final result is 14.   With what number did she start?

N290. What is the largest possible sum of two positive integers whose product is 100?

N291. A firefighter stood on the middle rung of a ladder, went up 3 rungs, was forced down 5 rungs, and then went up 7 rungs to extinguish the fire. Then the firefighter climbed the remaining 6 rungs to the top of the ladder. How many rungs are there on the entire ladder?

N292. If 3 **bads** = 10 **wickeds** and 6 **wickeds** = 9 **means**, how many **means** does it take to equal 2 **bads**?

N293. A grocer bought 15 dozen oranges at $1.00 a dozen. She threw away 20 rotten oranges, and then sold the rest at 8 oranges for 85¢. How much profit did the grocer make?

N294. Given $f(x) = (x-1)^3$ and $g(x) = \dfrac{x^2-1}{2x+1}$. Find $g(f(3))$.

N295. Four people can be seated at a single card table. If two tables are placed end to end, six people can be seated as shown in the diagram at the right. How many tables must be placed end to end to seat 22 people?

N296. X = $.5\overline{09}$ and Y = $.21\overline{6}$, Find X + Y expressed as a fraction in simplest form.

N297. The numerator of a fraction is 3 less than the denominator. If 39 is added to the numerator and 4 is subtracted from the denominator the resulting number is 11. Find the original fraction.

N298. Suppose that a, b, and c represent 1, 2, and 3
in some order. What is the largest possible sum
that can result in the addition problem at the right?

<pre>
    abc4
    5abc
+   cb6a
</pre>

N299. A basketball team won 40% of its first 15 games. Beginning with the sixteenth game, how many consecutive games does the team have to win in order to have a 55% winning record?

N300. The number of bacteria in a colony that is growing in a lab doubles every six hours. If there are 2,550 bacteria at 6 AM on Monday, how many bacteria will there be at noon on Tuesday.

N301. How many different natural numbers between 10 and 200 have the sum of their digits equal to 6, if zero is not a digit of any of the numbers?

N302. Twenty-four hamsters weigh the same as 18 guinea pigs. Assuming all hamsters weigh the same amount and all guinea pigs weigh the same amount, how many hamsters weigh the same as 24 guinea pigs?

N303. Find all values of d so that 27296958573653d is divisible by 6.

N304. Change 143 to a Base Two (Binary) numeral.

N305. The Pin Number for my Swiss bank account is a 4 digit number written as four binary numerals. What is my Pin Number if the binary numerals are: $0011 - 1001 - 0101 - 0110$?

N306. Find the sum of the first 300 multiples of three.

N307. What is the unit's digit of $2^{93} + 3^{91}$?

N308. The numerator of a fraction is 4 less than the denominator. If the numerator is increased by twenty-five and the denominator is decreased by 4, the resulting number is 6. What is the original fraction?

N309. A Δ B = B − 2A + 3. Find the value of 2 Δ 6.

N310. If A Δ B = B − 2A + 3, find all values of x such that x Δ 9 = 0.

N311. Find the product of all fractions in the form $\dfrac{n}{n+1}$ where n is integer and $20 \le n < 100$.

N312. Using nickels, dimes, and quarters, how many different ways can you have exactly 50 cents?

N313. The numerator of a fraction is 3 less than the denominator. If the numerator is increased by 17 and the denominator is decreased by 6, the resulting number is 5. What is the original fraction?

N314. Given the sequence: 32, 25, 18, 11, ... Find the 337th term.

N315. Given set W = $\left\{ -1.4, \ \dfrac{4}{3}, \ \dfrac{11}{8}, \ -\dfrac{3}{2}, \ -2\dfrac{2}{3} \right\}$. Arrange the elements in this set from smallest to largest and find the product of the second and fourth terms in this ordered set of elements.

N316. Find the sum of: $1 + 2 + 3 + \ldots + 199 + 200 + 199 + \ldots + 3 + 2 + 1$.

N317. Brooke is in a hot air balloon that has just taken off and is now floating 56 meters above it launching point. Oscar is standing on the ground, 42 meters away from the launching point. How far apart are Brooke and Oscar?

N318. Find the next number in the sequence: 6, 9, 18, 39, 78, ...

N319. On his birthday, Sean was 14 years old and his father was 41. Sean noticed that his age was his father's age with the digits reversed. How many years later will their ages next have their digits reversed?

N320. Sue and her five sisters are at an amusement park. They decide to pair up for the roller-coaster rides so that each person will ride with each other person. How many rides must be taken?

N321. Given $A = \{a, \ b, \ c, \ d\}$. List all the subsets of A that have a cardinality of three.

N322. What is the unit's digit of $7^{31} + 3^{33}$?

N323. What is the smallest positive number that leaves a remainder of 2 when the number divided by 3, 4, or 5?

N324. Write 3494 as a Roman numeral.

N325. Find the Least Common Multiple of 165 and 450.

N326. A clock is set correctly at 1:00 PM. If it loses 3 minutes every hour, what will the clock show when the correct time is 10:00 AM the next day?

N327. Find the Greatest Common Factor of 22050, 4620.

N328. Find d so that 57663972513878d is divisible by 11.

N329. How many different whole numbers are factors of 100?

N330. Find d so that 57663972513878d is divisible by 4.

N331. Find d so that 57663972513878d is divisible by 6.

N332. Faith baked at least 6 dozen cookies but fewer than 100 cookies. If she divides the cookies evenly among 7 plates, 4 cookies are left over. If she divides the cookies evenly among 6 plates, 5 cookies are left over. How many cookies did Faith bake?

N333. In a four digit number, the sum of the thousands and hundreds digit is 3. The tens digit is 4 times the hundreds digit. The ones digit is seven more than the thousands digit. No two digits are equal. Find the 4 digit number.

N334. Simplify: $2\sqrt{363} + 3\sqrt{180} - 3\sqrt{243}$

N335. Find all the common factors of 154 and 252.

N336. Write 2944 as a Roman numeral.

N337. Given the sequence 32, 25, 18, 11, . . . Find the 137th term.

N338. Simplify: $\dfrac{\sqrt{2^6 + 2^6 + 2^6 + 4^3}}{\sqrt[3]{6 \times 15 \times 300}}$.

N339. Craig has had his dog since it was a puppy. He said. If you multiply my dog's age by 4, and then divide by 12, you get 5. How old is Craig's dog?

N340. Change 138 to a binary numeral.

N341. If $20 \times 40 \times 80 \times 160 = (2^x)(5^y)$, find x + y.

N342. Given that x and y are positive integers. xy = 24. $\dfrac{xy}{x-y}$ is a positive integer. Find x and y.

N343. The Fleet Street condominium complex has between 1 and 15 condos, numbered 1. 2, 3, etc. Alex lives in one of these condos. The sum of all the condo numbers less than his equals the sum if all the condo numbers greater than his. How many condos are in this condominium complex.

N344. Find the sum of the first 300 multiples of two.

N345. What is the value of: $0.\overline{1} + 0.\overline{2} + 0.\overline{3} + 0.\overline{4}$.

N346. Annie has a silver dollar, a half dollar, a quarter, a dime, and a nickel. After losing one of her coins, she has exactly seven times as much money as her brother had. Which coin did Annie lose?

N347. A company makes 4080 ice cream sandwiches in an eight hour day. These ice cream sandwiches are packed 24 to a case. How many cases are produced from Monday through Sunday if Saturday and Sunday are twelve hour work days but the production rate is the same as it is on weekdays?

N348. Write 23 as the sum of 3 different prime numbers in two different ways.

N349. Find X in the series, 2, 6, 12, 20, X, 42, 56.

N350. Express in simplest form: $\left(1 - \dfrac{1}{3}\right)\left(1 - \dfrac{1}{4}\right)\left(1 - \dfrac{1}{5}\right)\left(1 - \dfrac{1}{50}\right)$.

N351. Replace $\square$ with a whole number so that the statement $\dfrac{3}{5} < \dfrac{\square}{7} < \dfrac{4}{5}$ is true.

N352. What is the smallest natural number that is a multiple of each number from 1 to 10?

N353. The whole number W is divisible by 7. W leaves a remainder of 1 when divided by 2, 3, 4, or 5. What is the smallest value that W can be?

N354. What is the smallest prime number that will divide $7^{13} + 11^{25}$?

N355. How many multiples of 7 are there between 100 and 1000?

N356. Given the sequence 9, 31, 60, 103, 167, find the next term.

N357. Find sum of the common factors of 56 and 168.

N358. After a $14\frac{2}{3}\%$ discount, a house alarm system was priced at $1792. What was the original price?

N359. A machine makes 5 bottle caps in 22 seconds. How many bottle caps can it make in 66 minutes?

N360. Five friends (Al, Ben, Carl, Don, Ernie) sit in a circle in alphabetical order and begin to count down to 1. Al starts by saying "34", followed by Ben saying "33", and so on. Continuing around the circle, which one of the friends says "1"?

N361. What part of three-fourths is one-tenth?

N362. How many positive integers less than 100 can be written as the product of the first two powers of two different prime numbers?

N363. A group consists of 2 girls for every boy. 24 more girls joined the group. There are now 5 girls for every boy. How many boys are in the group?

N364. The average of four consecutive even integers is 17. Find the largest of the four integers.

N365. You purchase a car for $25,300. It will decrease in value by 10% each year. What is the value of the car (correct to whole dollars) three years from now?

N366. Express the decimal $0.5\overline{3}$ as a fraction in simplest form.

N367. A car was purchased for \$27528 and it included a sales tax of $6\frac{2}{7}\%$. What was the cost of the car?

N368. A four-digit number is written on a piece of paper and Lee accidently spills grape juice on the number so that the last two digits are no longer visible. The number with just the visible digits is now 86? The four-digit number is divisible by 3, by 4, and by 5. Find the four-digit number.

N369. Express $\frac{1}{3} \times 0.32 + \frac{2}{3} \times 0.64 + \frac{4}{3} \times 0.32$ as a fraction in simplest form.

N370. Simplify: $\dfrac{8! \times 9! \times 15!}{11! \times 10! \times 12!}$.

N371. Find the sum of the first 350 natural numbers.

N372. 14 can be express as the sum of two prime numbers in exactly two different ways: 11 + 3 = 14 and 7 + 7 = 14. In how many ways can 40 be expressed as the sum of two prime numbers?

N373. Express: $\dfrac{1}{100} + \dfrac{2}{100} + \dfrac{3}{100} + \dfrac{996}{100} + \dfrac{997}{100} + \dfrac{998}{100}$ as a decimal.

N374. Sara writes the natural numbers in four columns A, B, C, D, as shown at the right. If she continues in the same manner the number 100 will appear in the column headed by which letter?

A	B	C	D
1	2	3	4
8	7	6	5
9	10	11	12
16	15	14	13

N375. Express 4% X 4% as a percent.

N376. Change $28\frac{3}{4}\%$ to a simplified fraction.

N377. A famous sequence begins: 1, 1, 2, 3, 5, 8, 13, 21, 34, 55, and so on. Each term of the sequence after the second term is the sum of the previous two terms. The eleventh term is 34 + 55 or 89. How many of the first thirty terms of this sequence are odd numbers?

N378. Six girls form a basketball team but only five can play at one time. They enter a tournament of 30 games. They arrange for each of the six girls to play the same number of complete games. How many complete games will each girl play?

N379. If x and y are positive integers, what is the least value for x and y such that $\dfrac{1}{640} = \dfrac{x}{10^y}$?

N380. Janice goes to the Perfectly Pampered Salon for a 1 PM haircut appointment. The salon technician cuts at the rate of 109 hairs per second. Assuming that Janice has 98,100 hairs on her head, at what time will she be finished with her haircut?

N381. A bike shop has the following advertisement:
     9:00 AM: 10% of originally marked prices
     10:00 AM: 10% of 9:00 AM prices
     11:00 AM: 10% of 10:00 AM prices
At 12:15 PM, Kate bought a bike with an originally marked price of $400. What did Kate finally pay for the bike?

N382. Courtney wrote a list of 2000 consecutive odd integers. By how much would the largest number on her list exceed the smallest number on her list?

N383. Change $6\dfrac{7}{8}\%$ to a simplified fraction.

N384. If $a = 2^8 3^4 19^2 7$ and $b = 2^5 3^2 19$, express $\dfrac{(9b)^2}{a}$ in simplest form.

N385. The first three terms of a geometric sequence are: $\dfrac{16}{15}, \dfrac{8}{6}, \dfrac{5}{3}, \ldots$ Find the rational number in simplest form that is the sixth term.

N386. Change $\dfrac{11}{4}$ to a percent.

N387. Arrange the elements in Set A in order from smallest to largest: $A = \left\{ \dfrac{5}{8}, \dfrac{8}{15}, \dfrac{7}{12}, \dfrac{9}{16} \right\}$.

N388. After a $16\dfrac{1}{4}\%$ discount, a new HDTV was priced at $1340. What was the original price?

N389. Fred Flintstone was immortalized for his phrase YABBADABBADOO. If this phrase was repeated over and over, what letter will be in the 275th position?

N390. Of 75 cars that were inspected, 12 needed brake repair and 18 needed exhaust system repair. If the brakes or exhaust system on 50 of the cars did not need repair, how many cars needed both brake and exhaust system repairs?

N391. You are buying shampoo and you want the best buy for the same product. Item A is priced at $2.88 for 12 ounces and Item B is priced at $5.17 for 22 ounces. Which item is the best value?

N392. 75% of 76 is the same as 95% of what whole number?

N393. A student mistakenly multiplied a positive number by 10 , when he should have divided the original positive number by 10. The answer he found was 33.66 more than the answer he should have found. Find the original positive number.

N394. Order the following set from smallest to largest $\left\{ \dfrac{.06}{8}, \dfrac{.08}{6}, \dfrac{8}{.06}, \dfrac{6}{.08}, \dfrac{.08}{.06} \right\}$ and find the product of the first term and the fifth term.

N395. A rock group called the After Glows will be playing a concert at the Columbia Memorial Auditorium and it is anticipated that all 2000 reserved seats and 8000 general admission seats will be sold. The total expenses for the After Glows appearance $420,000. The promoter for this concert has decided to charge $75 for reserved seats and $40 for general admission. What is the promoter's expected profit for this concert?

N396. Mark took a test and on the first 20 questions, he got twelve of them correct and eight of them wrong. On the remaining questions he got twice as many wrong as he got correct. He ended up getting one-half of the total questions on the test correct. How many questions were on the test?

N397. One lighthouse's light flashes every 10 seconds. A second lighthouse's light flashes every 12 seconds and a third lighthouse's light flashes every 18 seconds. How many times between midnight and 6 AM inclusive do they flash at the same time assuming that a midnight they flash simultaneously?

N398. Over a period of five games, a basketball team made exactly 44% of their shots. The number of shots taken was more than 310 but less than 350. How many shots were made?

N399. The cost including a $6\dfrac{1}{4}\%$ sales tax for a Ford Focus is $26,350. What is the original price of this car?

N400. After a $15\frac{3}{4}\%$ discount, a house alarm system was priced at \$2696. What was the original price?

N401. A car was purchased for \$25259 and it included a sales tax of $7\frac{5}{7}\%$. What was the cost of the car?

N402. Find the smallest natural number which when divided by 6 gives a remainder of 1, and when divided by 11 gives a remainder of 6.

N403. The sequence 2, 3, 5, 6, 7, 10, . . . consists of all natural numbers which are neither perfect squares or perfect cubes. Find the 75th term of this sequence.

N404. How many three-digit positive integers can be written using only odd integers?

N405. What is 5% of 5% of 4% expressed as a percent?

N406. If $g(x) = \dfrac{x^2 - 1}{2x + 1}$, find $g\left(\dfrac{3}{5}\right)$.

N407. Change $\dfrac{7}{16}$ to a percent.

N408. Carl the cableman has a blue cable wire that is 525 inches long and a gray cable wire that is 945 inches long. What is the length of the longest piece he can cut from both cables so that these smaller pieces are the same length and all the wires are used? How many pieces of cable wire will Carl have?

N409. Given the sequence: $\dfrac{16}{15}, \dfrac{8}{6}, \dfrac{5}{3}$. Find the seventh term and express it as the ratio of two integers.

N410. The pages of a book are numbered consecutively starting with page 1. 258 digits are used to number all these pages. What is the last page number?

N411. On Jeopardy, each contest matches three people. In a tournament, in each match there is always one winner. The winner advances to the next round while the other two are eliminated. The tournament continues until one person remains. If 243 players enter the tournament, compute the number of contests that must be played to determine the champion.

N412. Simplify: $\left(\dfrac{3}{2}\right)^{-2}\left(\dfrac{3^{-1}+2^{-3}}{6^{-1}-4^{-1}}\right)$.

N413. Express $\dfrac{\left(a^2b^3c^2\right)^5}{\left(a^3b^2c^3\right)(abc)^2}$ in simplest form and with positive exponents.

N414. Simplify: $7+6\left[9-2(4-7)^2\right]\div 3$.

N415. Find three multiples of 420 and 36 that are larger than 3000.

N416. Peg has made 12 cups of punch by using 3 parts lemonade, 2 parts ginger ale, and 1 part root beer. Molly drinks one cup of punch then realizes that Peg needs a full 12 cups of this punch. Molly tries to help by adding 1 cup of ginger ale to the pitcher of punch. What is the ratio of the three ingredients in the punch using whole numbers for all parts of the ratio?

N417. Find all common factors of 84 and 112.

N418. Express $T=\overline{369}$ in simplest rational form.

N419. If $5^n=2$. What is the value of 25^{2n+1}.

N420. Express $\left(1+\dfrac{1}{3}\right)\left(1+\dfrac{1}{4}\right)\left(1+\dfrac{1}{5}\right)\cdots\left(1+\dfrac{1}{49}\right)\left(1+\dfrac{1}{50}\right)$ in simplest form.

N421. Find the 14th term of 24, 12, 6, 3, . . . Express it as a simplified rational number.

N422. For positive numbers a and b, the positive difference of a and b is divided by the positive difference of their reciprocals and the result is 5. What is the product of a and b?

N423. Three warning lights flash continuously every 45 minutes, 60 minutes and 75 minutes. If they flash at the same time at midnight on Sunday, how many times until midnight Saturday night will they flash simultaneously?

N424. Simplify: $\left(\dfrac{6^{-1}}{2^{-3}}\right)\left(\dfrac{4^{-1}-3^{-2}}{8^{-1}+3^{-2}}\right)$.

N425. What is the ratio of $3\frac{1}{2}$ yd to 78 inches?

N426. The product of two numbers is 9 and their sum is 12. Express their positive difference in simplest radical form.

N427. In 2020 a car was purchased for \$25,302. If the car depreciates in value by 10% each year, what will be the value of the car (correct to cents) when it will have been driven for 3 years?

N428. Tina bought a box of dog biscuits for her dog Karma. She gave Karma 3 biscuits each day for 10 consecutive days. Then she counted 96 biscuits left in the box. At this rate, for how many weeks will a full box of biscuits feed Karma?

N429. The ratio of John's allowance to Bill's allowance is 3:7. The ratio of John's allowance to Mary's allowance is 2:5. What is the ratio of Mary's allowance to Bill's allowance?

N430. What is the simplified numerical value of $\dfrac{a+11b}{a-b}$ if $\dfrac{4a+3b}{a-2b}=5$?

N431. Find the sum x + y in simplest form if x = $.5\overline{09}$ and y = $.21\overline{6}$. .

N432. Given: −34, −28, −22, ... Find the 287th term of this sequence.

N433. If $f(x)=7x+b$ and $g(x)=3x+d$ and $f(g(x))=g(f(x))$. Determine the value of $\dfrac{b}{d}$.

N434. A set has 5 elements. How many subsets does it have?

N435. The numerator of a fraction is 4 less than the denominator. If the numerator is increased by 17 and the denominator is decreased by 3, the resulting number is 5. Find the original fraction.

N436. Given 78453393261366F. Find F so that the number is divisible by 6.

N437. Positive integers a, b, and c satisfy the following conditions:

GCF(a, b, c) = 1
GCF(a, b) = 3
GCF(a, c) = 4
GCF(b, c) = 5

What is the least possible value of LCM(a, b, c)?

N438. Given 78453393261366F. Find F so that the number is divisible by 11.

N439. Simplify: $\dfrac{7^{-2}}{5^{-1}}\left(\dfrac{56^{-1}+7^{-1}}{2^{-2}+3^{-1}}\right)$

N440. X = $.5\overline{09}$ and Y = $.2\overline{16}$, Find X + Y expressed as a fraction in simplest form.

N441. If$(a)(b) = 168$, $(b)(c) = 54$, $(a)(c) = 63$, express the value of $(a)(b)(c)$ in simplest form.

N442. Express $\dfrac{2}{100} + \dfrac{3}{100} + \dfrac{4}{100} + \; + \dfrac{997}{100} + \dfrac{998}{100} + \dfrac{999}{100}$ as a decimal.

N443. How many positive integers less than 100 can be written as the product of the first two powers of two different prime numbers.

N444. On Thursday Kyle ate 20% of the jellybeans in the bowl. Friday, he ate $\dfrac{2}{5}$ of what was left. What percent of the jellybeans in the bowl did Kyle eat in those two days?

N445. Find the sum of the factors of 5! .

N446. Express n = $0.\overline{693}$ as a rational number in simplest form.

N447. Jack has a herd of cattle. Then he bought more cattle so that his total was four times the original amount. He was then given six more cattle, he then sold half the herd and finally lost 4 cattle. At this time, Jack had 39 cattle. How many cattle did Jack have at the start?

N448. If A = 2^{100} and B = 3^{100}, find $A \times B$.

N449. The sum of three numbers is 84. The ratio of the first to the second is 4:3. The ratio of the second to the third is 3:7. Find the three numbers?

N450. Suppose the positive odd numbers are grouped in the following way: {1}; {3, 5}; {7, 9, 11}; {13, 15, 17, 19}; . . . . What is the sum of the numbers in the tenth group?

N451. Consider the fractions $\dfrac{1}{6}$ and $\dfrac{1}{7}$. Which fraction is larger? Find three fractions that are between them.

N452. If X is the unit's digit of 12^{38} and Y is the unit's digit of 13^{42}, find X + Y.

N453. Express $0.1\overline{72}$ as a fraction in simplest form.

N454. Find all values of d so that 72296958573d68 is divisible by 8.

N455. Find a fraction that is between $\dfrac{1}{5}$ and $\dfrac{1}{4}$ but is closer to $\dfrac{1}{4}$.

N456. The train ride from Boston to NYC is 221 miles. Leaving at 7:30 AM at an average rate of 34 mph and stopping for 4 minutes at each of 10 stations, at what time will the train arrive in NYC?

N457. If 2 cows can be exchanged for 63 sheep and 2 rabbits can be exchanged for 3 chicken and 3 sheep can be exchanged for 32 rabbits, then 3 cows can be exchanged for how many chickens?

N458. Each of AB and DE represent a 2-digit number. Different letters represent different digits, chosen from 6, 7, 8, and 9. What is the largest product that AB X DE can have?

N459. Each of c and d are chosen from the set of whole numbers 1, 2, 3, . . . , 8, 9, 10. In how many different ways will $\dfrac{c}{d}$ have a value greater then $\dfrac{1}{2}$ and less than 1? Consider $\dfrac{2}{3}$ and $\dfrac{4}{6}$, for example, as two different ways.

N460. Find d so that 384692178925324d is divisible by 11.

N461. What is the ratio of 3 yards to 99 inches in simplest form?

N462. Find $5\dfrac{1}{7}\%$ of 5600.

N463. Simplify: $1 + 2 + 3 + \ldots + 198 + 199 + 200 + 199 + 198 + \ldots + 3 + 2 + 1$.

N464. Each of eight traffic lights on Main Street show green for 2 minutes, then switches to other colors. The traffic light turns green 10 seconds apart, from the first light to the eighth light. From the time that the first light turns green until it switches to another color, for how many seconds will all eight lights show green at the same time?

N465. The bottom line cost of a used Lexus is $21,897. This cost includes a $6\dfrac{1}{4}\%$ sales tax, a $2\dfrac{2}{9}\%$ delivery charge, and a $4\dfrac{1}{6}\%$ sales commission. What is the original cost of this used Lexus?

N466. At Boston's Museum of Science two film documentaries were being shown. One was 32 minutes long and the other was 40 minutes long. If both films are shown continuously and start at 10 AM and the closing time for the museum is 9:00 PM, how many times will these films start at the same time?

N467. Using pennies, nickels, and dimes, how many different ways can you make 25 cents.

N468. In Julianna's stamp collector's album, there are four 1¢ stamps, three 5¢ stamps, and three 25¢ stamps. How many different postage amounts of at least 1¢ can Julianna make?

N469. Simplify and express your answer with positive exponents: $\dfrac{\left(6m^3n^2\right)\left(5mn^4\right)}{\left(3mn\right)^2\left(25m^3n^2\right)}$.

N470. The sum of three numbers is 98. The ratio of the first to the second is 2:3. The ratio of the second to the third is 5:8. Find the three numbers?

N471. Find the sum of the first five hundred multiples of 2.

N472. Find d so that 384692178925324d is divisible by 6.

N473. Simplify $7 + 6\left[9 - 2(4 - 7)^2\right] \div 3$.

N474. Three warning lights flash continuously every 45 minutes, 60 minutes, and 75 minutes. If they flash at the same time at midnight on Sunday, how many times until midnight Saturday night will they flash simultaneously?

GEOMETRY AND MEASUREMENT

G001. Stacy is using 120 inches of wire to build two structures: (1) a rectangle that is five times as long as it is wide and; (2) a square whose side length is the same as the width of the rectangle. What will be the exact area of Stacy's square?

G002. Find the area of an isosceles triangle with sides 39 cm, 39 cm, and 30 cm.

G003. Points A, B, C and D are on a line. They are not necessarily in that order. Point A is between B and C. Point B is between A and D. Point D is to the left of C. List the points in order from left to right.

G004. If the lengths of the sides of a quadrilateral are: $\sqrt{1}$, $\sqrt{9}$, $\sqrt{9}$, $\sqrt{8}$, then the perimeter of the quadrilateral is:

G005. Each side of square ABCD is doubled in length to form square EFGH. The perimeter of EFGH is 264 cm. Find the area of ABCD.

G006. The length of the first side of a triangle is a whole number greater than 3. The second side is 3 inches longer than the first side, and the third side is 3 inches longer than the second. How many such triangles have perimeters less than 36 inches?

G007. A rectangle has a width of 2.5 ft and a perimeter of 13 ft. What is the area of the rectangle?

G008. The hypotenuse of a right triangle is one inch more than twice the length of the shorter leg. The longer leg is 2 inches shorter than the hypotenuse. Find the length of the hypotenuse.

G009. If a triangle with a base of 6 inches has the same area as a circle with a radius of 6 inches, what is the length of the altitude of the triangle expressed as an exact value?

G010. You have 420 feet of fencing. After fencing in a square region, you have 120 feet of fencing remaining.

G011. Find the area of a square with diagonal of length d.

G012. A wheel on Julian's wheelbarrow has a radius of 12 inches. Julian pushed the wheelbarrow so that the wheel rotated 5 times. How many inches (to the nearest inch) did the wheel travel in 5 rotations?

G013. In the figure at the right, BC = AD = 18 inches.
$m\angle BCA = 32; m\angle BAC = 28.$
Find the measure of $\angle ADC$.

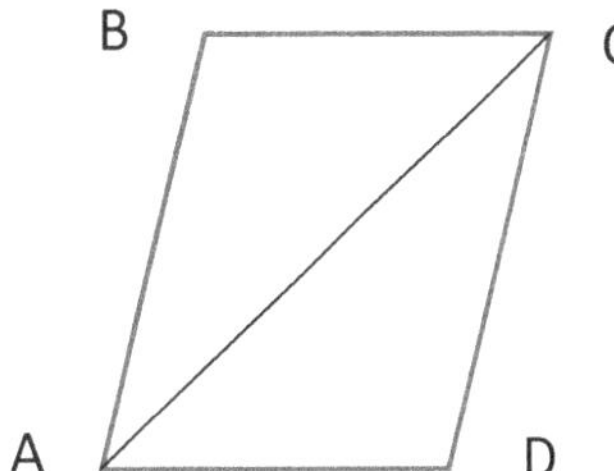

G014. The area of a rectangle in square inches is represented by the expression $x^2 + 2x - 8$. The length of the rectangle is x + 4 inches. What is an expression for the width of the rectangle in inches?

G015. At the right is an equilateral triangle
Inscribed in a circle of radius 2 cm.
Find the area of the region that is
outside the triangle but inside the
circle. Express the answer as an
exact value.

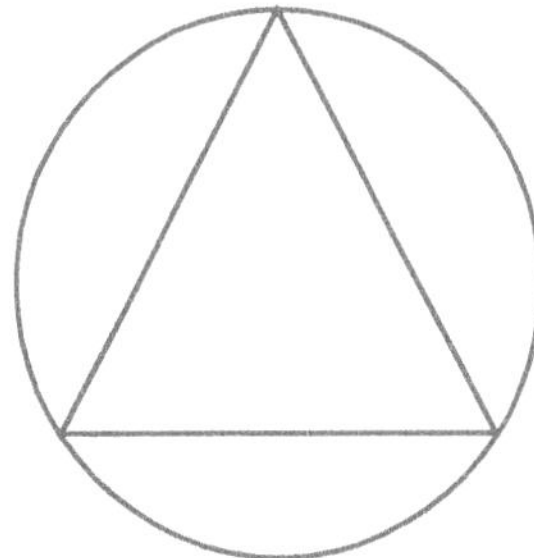

G016. A cube has sides that measure 4 cm. Find the total area of this figure.

G017. An angle is 3 more than half its supplement. Find both angles.

G018. The perimeter of a rectangle is 26 units. Each of the length and width of the rectangle is measured in natural numbers. What is the largest area in square units that the rectangle could have?

G019. Gil started walking at the Minuteman Statue on the Lexington Green. He walked 1.5 kilometers due east and then 2.0 kilometers due south. At the end of his walk, how far was Rick from his starting point at the statue?

G020. A rectangle has an area of 51 in^2 and a length of 10.2 inches. What is the perimeter of this rectangle?

G021. A closed rectangular box has a surface area of 1000 cm^2. Its length is twice its width, and its height is six times its width. What is the volume of this box?

G022. Two legs of a right triangle are x and (x − y), and the hypotenuse is (x + y). Find y in terms of x.

G023. One of two consecutive angles of a parallelogram is twice the other. The sides of the parallelogram are 8 cm and 12 cm. Express the area of this parallelogram as an exact value?

G024. An ant sits at vertex A of a cube with edge of length 1 foot. The ant moves along the edges of the cube and comes back to A with visiting any other point twice. Find the number of feet in the length of the longest such path.

G025. A circle has the same area as a square with side of length $\dfrac{1}{\pi}$. In terms of π, what is the diameter of the circle?

G026. A circle with radius 4 cm is inscribed in a square. Express the area outside the circle but inside the square as an exact value.

G027. A path 2 meters wide surrounds a rectangular garden 20 meters long and 12 meters wide. Find the area of the path.

G028. Given rectangle ABCD with AD = BC = 10 and AB = CD = 24. Point E lies on AB such that the ratio of AE:EB = 1:2. Find the perimeter of triangle DEB.

G029. Using $\pi = \dfrac{22}{7}$, a square prism with base edge of 28 cm and height 33 cm is melted down and recast as a cone with radius 14 cm. What is the height of the cone?

G030. Given $\triangle ABC$. D is a point on AC and $\overline{BD}$ is drawn. $\overline{AD} = \overline{BD} = \overline{BC}$. The measure of $\angle ADB$ is twice the measure of $\angle BDC$. What is the measure of $\angle ABC$?

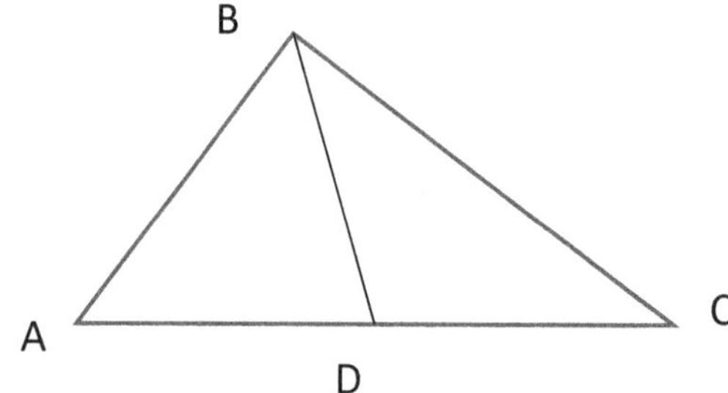

G031. Find the area of a rhombus with side 51 and shorter diagonal 48.

G032. Alex has 400 feet of fencing. What is the largest rectangular shaped pen he can make for his dog?

G033. If a square's perimeter is 84x, then its area is:

G034. Two smaller rectangles (measured in inches) with equal heights are cut from a rectangular piece of paper with dimensions 60 inches and 20 inches. The area of the remaining piece of paper is 980 in^2. Find the height of each cut out rectangle.

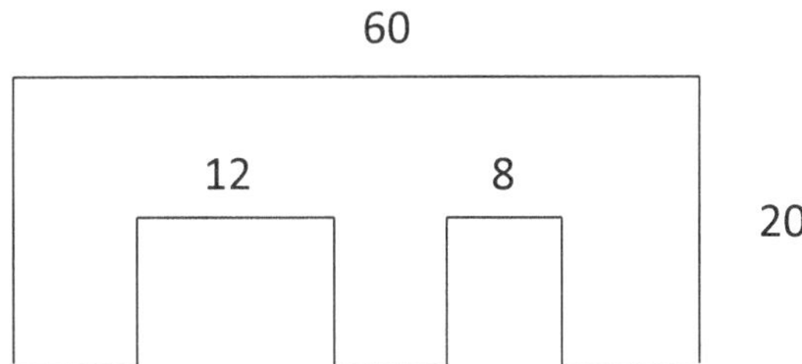

G035. Find the area of a parallelogram with adjacent sides of length 6 cm and 12 cm and the angle between the two adjacent sides is 60°.

G036. How many liters of paint are needed to paint the walls of a room 6 m long, 4 m wide and 2.5 m tall if one liter of paint covers 20m^2 . Assume that there are no doors and no windows.

G037. In the diagram at the right, AB = 4 cm, AD = 6 cm, and CD = 8 cm. Angles A and D are right angles Find the area of ABCD.

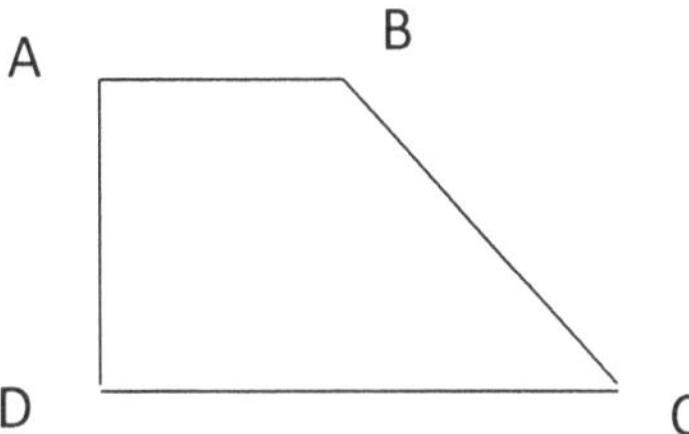

G038. A picture frame measures 20 cm by 30 cm. A blue border 5 cm wide will surround the picture that is inside the frame. Find the area of the blue border.

G039. A large rectangle is composed of five congruent smaller rectangles, each with whole number dimensions as shown at the right. If the perimeter of each smaller rectangle is 20 cm, find the area of the entire large rectangle.

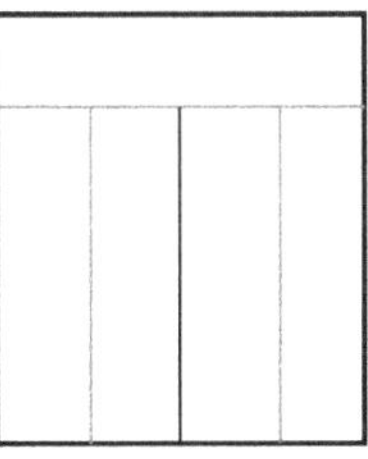

G040. In the figure at the right, $m\angle CBD = m\angle BCD = 60$. BC = 4, AD = 5, AB = 6. The perimeter of triangle ABD is how much greater than the perimeter of triangle BCD?

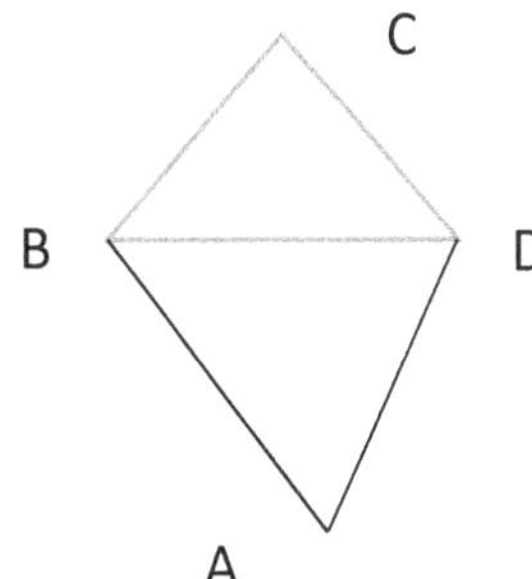

G041. Using the figure at the right, AD = BC = 13.
AB = 21, CD = 11. $DE \perp AB$ and $CF \perp AB$.
Find the length of DE.

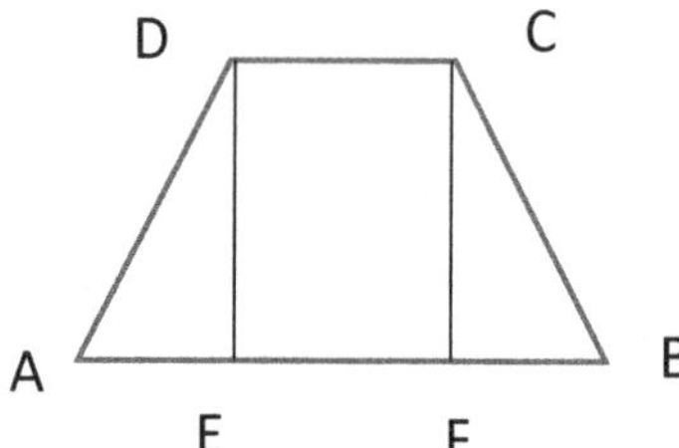

G042. A rectangular field is 60 feet longer than it is wide. A neighbor's fence borders the length of this field. How many yards of fencing are needed to fence the other three sides if the area of the field is 72,000 ft²?

G043. Given rectangle ABCD with E the midpoint of $\overline{AB}$. AD = BC = 5 and AB = CD = 12. Find the area of $\triangle DEB$.

G044. In a closed rectangular box, the length is $\dfrac{3}{2}$ times the width. The height is $\dfrac{5}{4}$ times the length. Find the volume of this box if the total surface area of the box is 79,200 in² .

G045. A solid metal cylinder with radius 6 cm and height 18 cm is melted down and recast as a solid cone with radius 9 cm. Find the height of the cone.

G046. The sum of the measures of the interior angles of a regular polygon is 2340°. Find the measure of each interior angle of this polygon. Find the measure of each exterior angle at each vertex of this polygon.

G047. At the right is isosceles triangle ACD. $\overline{AB}$ is the perpendicular bisector of $\overline{CD}$. AC = 6x – 2,
AD = $\dfrac{1}{2}x + 9$, BD = 2y – 5, BC = $\dfrac{1}{4}y + 9$.
Find x and y.

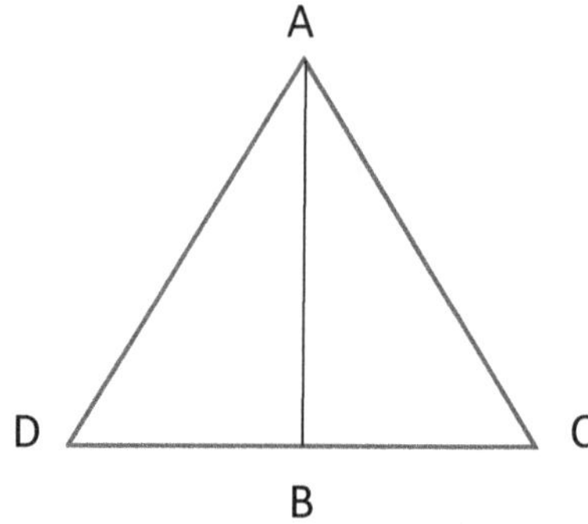

G048. Using the figure at the right:
Chords $\overline{AB}$ and $\overline{CD}$ intersect at E.
$m\overarc{AC} = 40$ and $m\overarc{BD} = 28$.
Find $m\angle AEC$.

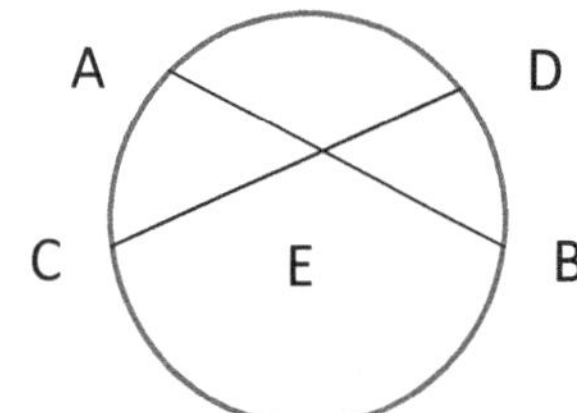

G049. In a rectangular coordinate system, what is the length of the line segment whose endpoints are (−7, −8) and (3, 16)?

G050. The volume of a cylinder is 72π. If the height of the cylinder is 8, find the lateral area (in terms of π) of the cylinder.

G051. Each side of a square is 6 feet in length. A rectangle has a width of 3 feet, and the same area as the square. Find the perimeter of the rectangle expressed in feet.

G052. The width of a rectangle is equal to the side length of a square. If the ratio of the area of the square to the area of the rectangle is 1:3 and the length of the rectangle is 15 ft, what is the side length of the square?

G053. A rectangle is twice as long as it is wide. The numerical value of its area in square feet is triple the numerical value of its perimeter, in feet. Find the perimeter of the rectangle.

G054. An isosceles trapezoid has base angles that measure 60°. The upper base is 8 cm and one of the equal sides is 10 cm. Find the perimeter of this polygon.

G055. What is the area of the triangle whose vertices have the coordinates (0,50), (50,0), and (50, 50)?

G056. The area of triangle ABC is 50 ft². Point D lies on side $\overline{AB}$ as shown at the right, with AD = 6 ft and AB = 25 ft. Find the area of triangle CBD.

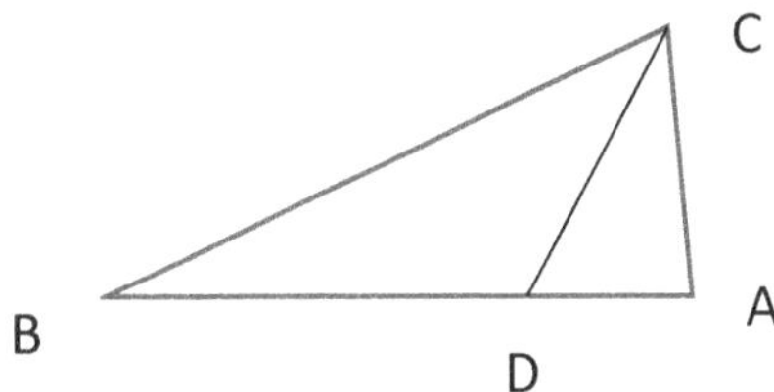

G057. Express the area that lies between two concentric circles with radii 3 cm and 4 cm as an exact value.

G058. At the right is parallelogram ABCD. The figure is divided into 4 identical nonoverlapping parallelograms. If each side of ABCD is 12, what is the perimeter of ABEF?

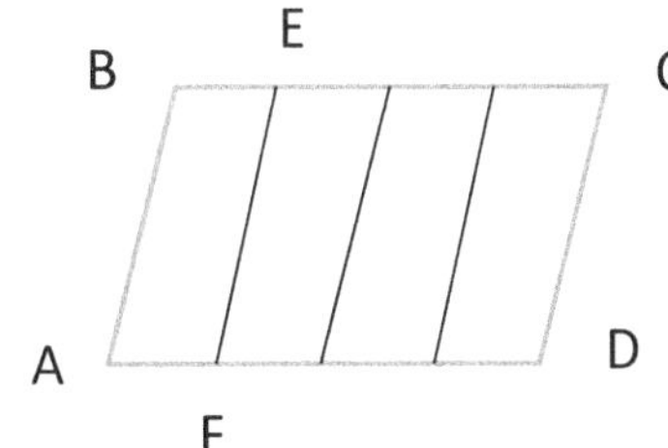

G059. Given square ABCD with sides 6 feet. E is on AD 4 feet from A. F is on CD 2 feet from C. What part of the square is the quadrilateral EBFD?

G060. Which of the following sets of centimeter units cannot be the lengths of a right triangle?   A = {8, 15, 17}, B = {0.6, 0.8, 1}, C. = {15, 39, 36}, D = {0.2, 0.5, 0.7}.

G061. Nolan has 42 identical cubes, each with 1-cm edges. He glues them together to form a rectangular solid. If the perimeter of the base is 18 cm, find the height of the rectangular solid.

G062. At the right is square ABCD whose Sides are each 2 units long. The length of the shortest path from A to C following the lines of the diagram is 4 units. How many different shortest paths are there from A to C?

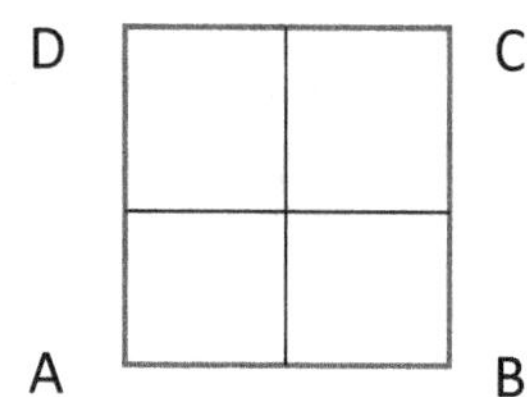

G063. Find the area of an isosceles trapezoid with equal sides of 39 and bases of 62 and 32.

G064. The area of each of two rectangles is 360 cm^2. The length of the second rectangle is 12 cm greater than the first , and its width is 5 cm less than the first. What is the difference of the perimeters of the two rectangles if the lengths and widths are positive integers?

G065. On line segment $\overline{ABCDE}$, D is the midpoint of $\overline{AE}$. The length of $\overline{BC}$ is $\dfrac{1}{3}$ the length of $\overline{AB}$, and $BC = CD$. What percent of AE is AC?

G066. The second side of a triangle is twice the length of the first side. The third side of the triangle is 6 cm longer than the second side. Determine the length of each side of this triangle if the perimeter is 66 cm.

G067. Using $\pi = \dfrac{22}{7}$, a bicycle tire has a diameter of 28 inches. How many feet (correct to tenths) does it travel in 1000 revolutions of the tire?

G068. A triangle has sides 26 cm, 20 cm, 26 cm. Find the area of this triangle.

G069. Find the lateral area and total area of a triangular prism with sides 24 cm, 70 cm, 74 cm and height 13 cm.

G070. A circle and a square have equal areas. Find the ratio of the length of a side of the square to the length of a diameter of the circle.

G071. The cube shown at the right has a different whole number from 1 through 6 written on each of its faces. The sum of the numbers on each pair of opposite faces equals 7. Find the smallest possible values of A + B.

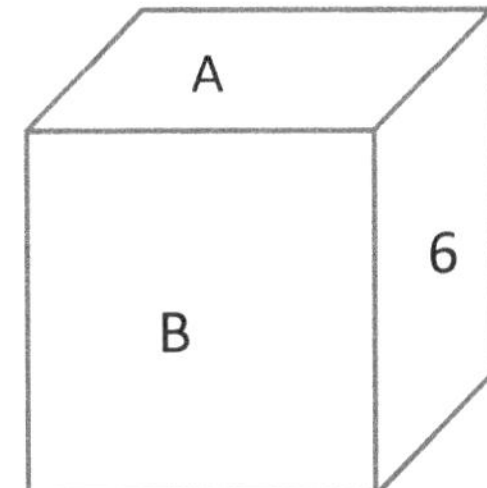

G072. A solid metal cylinder with radius 6 inches and height 18 inches is melted down and recast as a cone with radius 9 inches. Find the height of the cone.

G073. The dimensions of a 40 foot by 25 foot rectangle are each increased by 20%. The area of the original rectangle is what fractional part of the new rectangle?

G074. Using the figure at the right, Quadrilateral ACDE is similar to quadrilateral ABGF. $\overline{AE}$ = 15 in., $\overline{ED}$ = 11 in., $\overline{CD}$ = 12 in., $\overline{BF}$ = 12 in., $\overline{AB}$ = 8 in. Find the length of $\overline{AF}$.

G075. The diagonals of a rectangle intersect at a point 8 inches from the vertices. The diagonals also divide the angles of the rectangle in 30° and 60° angles. Find the lengths of the sides of the rectangle.

G076. Find the area of a rhombus with a 120° angle and perimeter 72 ft.

G077. Draw a circle around
Quadrilateral ABCD.
Label $m\overset{\frown}{DC}=48$,
$m\overset{\frown}{AB}=84$, $m\overset{\frown}{DAB}=184$.
Find the measure of
angles A, B, C, D

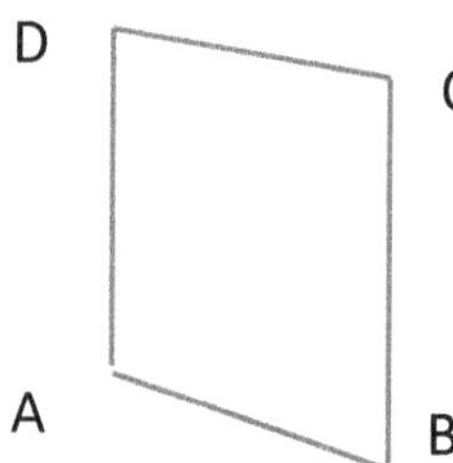

G078. A cone has a height of 48 cm and a radius of 15 cm. The cylinder's height is one-half that of the cone and the radius is twice that of the cone. Express the ratio of the volumes of the cone to the cylinder in simplest form.

G079. A rectangle with length 16 m and width 12 m is inscribed in a circle. Find the area of the region inside the circle but outside the rectangle. Express the answer as an exact value.

G080. (–9, 2), (–3, –12), (5, –3), and (–3, 6) are vertices of a quadrilateral. Find its area.

G081. A right triangular prism has base edges 15 in, 36 in, 39 in, and a volume of 45,900 in³. Find the height of the prism.

G082. Find the measure of an angle whose supplement is 16 less than three times its compliment.

G083. D, E, and F are collinear. E is between D and F. DE = 3y – 1, EF = y + 5, and DF = 20. Determine the length of DE.

G084. At the right, quadrilateral ABCD is inscribed in the circle, $m\overset{\frown}{DC}\ =\ 48, m\overset{\frown}{AB}\ =\ 84, m\overset{\frown}{DAB}\ =\ 184$. Find the measure of angles A and B.

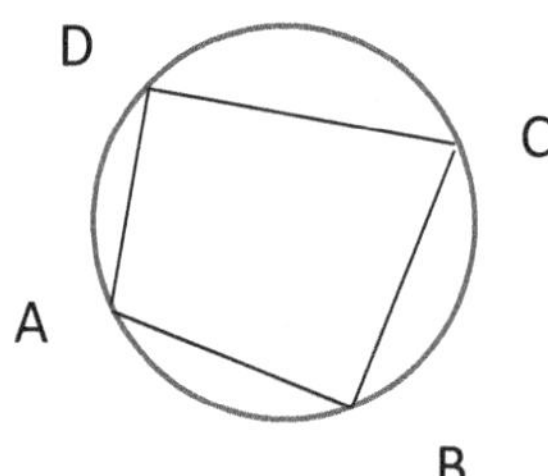

G085. At the right, a "tower" is formed by placing a small square on top of a large square. The perimeter of the tower is 52 inches and the perimeter of the large square is 40 inches. Find the perimeter of the small square.

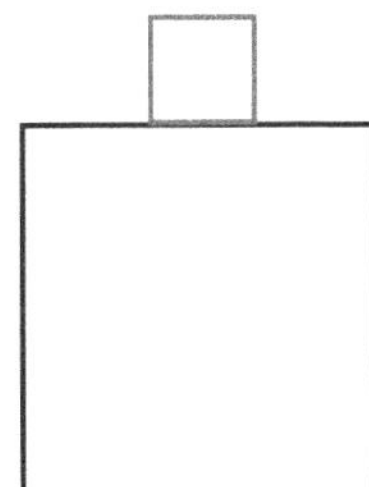

G086. Find the area of a rhombus with side 17 m and longer diagonal 30 m.

G087. Find the area of an isosceles right triangle with hypotenuse 20 in.

G088. A closed cylindrical shaped container has diameter 10 cm and height 4 cm. Find the lateral area, total area, and volume of this cylinder. Express the answers as exact values.

G089. (−3, −4), (−2, 6), (3, 2), (−11, 2) are vertices of a quadrilateral. Find its area.

G090. Find the area, expressed as an exact value, of a parallelogram with sides 6 ft and 12 ft and included angle of 60°.

G091. The perimeter of a rectangle is 22 cm and the area is 24 cm^2. What is the smallest integer dimension that the rectangle can have?

G092. Find the volume of a triangular prism with height 10 cm and base lengths 10 cm, 24 cm and 26 cm.

G093. On line segment $\overline{ABCDE}$, D is the midpoint of $\overline{AE}$. The length of $\overline{BC}$ is one third the length of $\overline{AB}$, and BC = BD. What percent of AE is AC?

G094. Find the area, expressed as an exact value, of a rhombus with an angle that measures 45° and a side of length 6 cm.

G095. Find the area, expressed as an exact value, of an isosceles trapezoid with base angles of 60°, non-parallel sides of 10 cm and upper base of 10 cm.

G096. At the right is rectangle ACDE.
BC = 2 cm, CD = 12 cm, DE = 8 cm, EF = 7 cm,
AF = 5 cm. Find the area of triangle BDF.

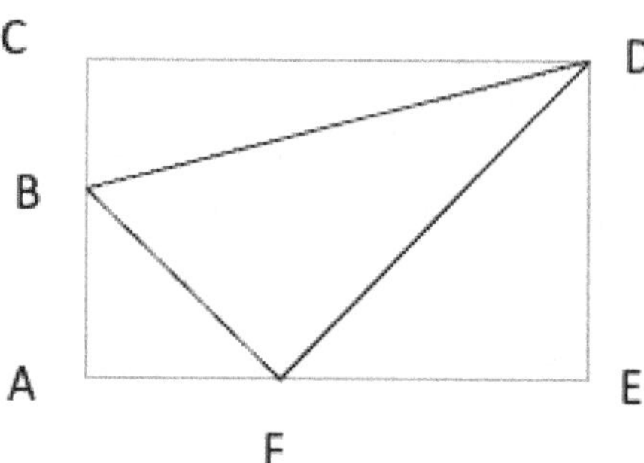

G097. The dimensions of a 40 ft by 25 ft rectangle are each increased 20%. The area of the original rectangle is what percent of the new rectangle expressed to the nearest whole number.

G098. At the right is square ABCD with Side 30 in. E is not the midpoint of $\overline{DC}$. Find the sum of the areas of $\triangle ADE$ and $\triangle BCE$.

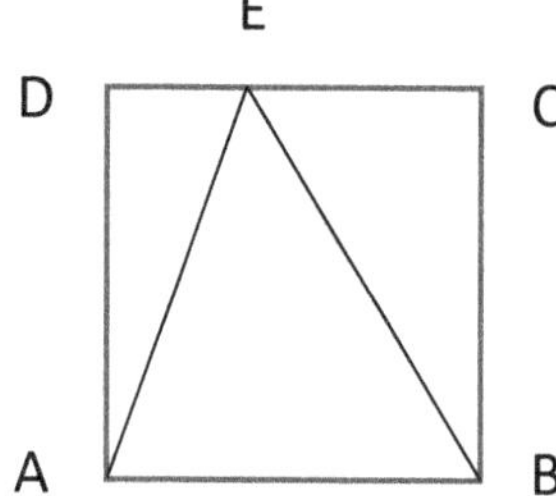

G099. Find the area of an isosceles trapezoid whose perimeter is 84 m and whose longer base is four times the length of the shorter base and the sum of the bases is 50 m.

G100. $\triangle ABC \sim \triangle XYZ.$ $m\angle A = m\angle X, m\angle B = m\angle Y, m\angle C = m\angle Z.$ AC = 12, AB = 8, BC = 16, and XY = 18. Find XZ and YZ.

G101. A cylindrical water tank is one-fifth full. If 3 liters of water were added, the tank would be one-fourth full. How many liters of water does the tank hold when it is full?

G102. Each side of the 9 ft by 9 ft square shown at The right is divided into three equal parts. Find the area of the octagonal shaped area that is inside the square.

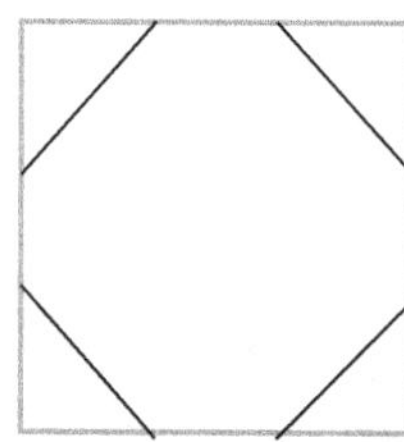

G103. Vin uses 11 toothpicks to form a row of 5 attached triangles as shown at the right. Suppose he continues this pattern, using 89 toothpicks in all. What is the total number of triangles formed?

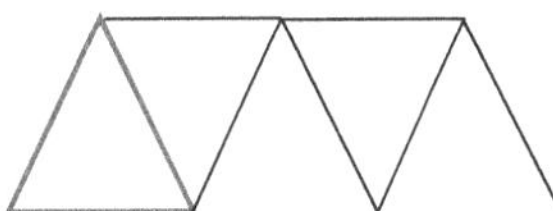

G104. John has an eight foot long piece of wire that he will cut and bend to make a frame for a right rectangular prism. The base of this prism is a square with side length 3 inches. Suppose John decides to build two identical prisms with the given dimensions of the base. What will be the total combined volume of these two rectangular prisms?

G105. An equilateral triangle is inscribed in a circle with radius 2 cm. Find the area, expressed as an exact value, of the region that is inside the circle but outside the triangle.

G106. A single story house is to be built on a rectangular plot of land 70 feet wide by 100 feet deep. The shorter side if this plot is along a street. The house must be set back 30 feet from the street. It must also be 20 feet from the back plot line and 10 feet from each side plot line. What is the largest area that this house can have?

G107. A container in the shape of a cylinder has a height of 48 cm and a radius of 15 cm. Another container in the shape of a cone has a height of 96 cm and a radius of 20 cm. Which container will hold more liquid and by how much (expressed as an exact value)?

G108. Equilateral triangle ABC has side length 400 cm and a perimeter equal to 100 times the perimeter of equilateral triangle DEF. How long is each side of triangle DEF?

G109. Find the area of a parallelogram with sides 36 inches and 44 inches that form a 30° angle.

G110. Two rectangular boxes have the same volume. One of the boxes is a cube and the other box has measurements of 8 feet by 4 feet by 16 feet. How long is an edge of the cube?

G111. At the right is quadrilateral DEFG
with altitude GH. $m\angle GDF = m\angle GFD = 45$.
$m\angle FDE = 30$, $m\angle DFE = 60$, $m\angle DEF = 90$.
$\overline{DG} = \overline{FG} = 22$.

Find $\overline{DF}$ and $\overline{DE}$.

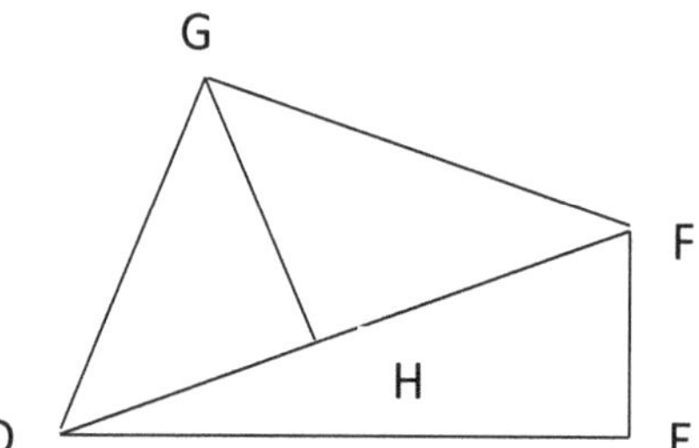

G112. A triangular piece is cut from a rectangular piece of paper 11 in by 12 in leaving a pentagon with four of its sides of length 5 in, 11 in, 12 in, and 7 in. Find the length of the missing side of the pentagon and find the area of the pentagon.

G113. Barney has 364 feet of fencing. After fencing in a square region, he has 160 feet of fencing remaining. What is the area of the square region?

G114. The scale drawing of a rectangular floor has a width of three-fourths inches and a length of two inches. If the actual width of the floor is 12 feet, what is the actual perimeter of the floor?

G115. A wire is attached from the ground 16 feet from the base of an upright utility pole to the top of the same utility pole at a point 30 feet above the ground. How long is the wire?

G116. What is the perimeter of the figure in feet of the figure at the right. All angles of this figure are right angles.

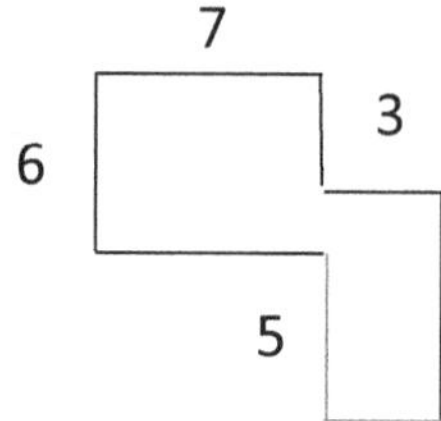

G117. Which holds more: A cylinder with radius 10 cm and height 30 cm or a cone with radius 15 cm and slant height 39 cm?

G118. Each side of square ABCD is doubled to form square EFGH. The perimeter of EFGH is 264 cm. What is the area of square ABCD?

G119. A rectangular floor measures 9 ft by 11ft and is covered completely by tiles. Each tile is either a 2 ft by 3 ft rectangle or a square 1 ft on a side. No tiles overlap. What is the least total number of tiles that could have been used to cover the floor?

G120. Marissa's rectangular garden and Kaylee's rectangular garden each have the same area of 36 m^2. Each side is measured in whole meters. Marissa's garden is 1 m wider than Kaylee's garden, but Kaylee's garden is 3 m longer than Marissa's garden. How wide is Marissa's garden?

G121. Find the area of a regular hexagon with perimeter 24 inches. Express the answer as an exact value.

G122. A garden measures 10 feet by 20 feet and it is enclosed by a side 2 foot wide sidewalk. Find the area of the sidewalk.

G123. Using the figure at the right, $m\angle AOE = 2x - 4$, $m\angle EOZ = 3x$, $\overline{OB}$ bisects $\angle AOC$, $\overline{BZ}$ and $\overline{EC}$ intersect at O. Solve for x.

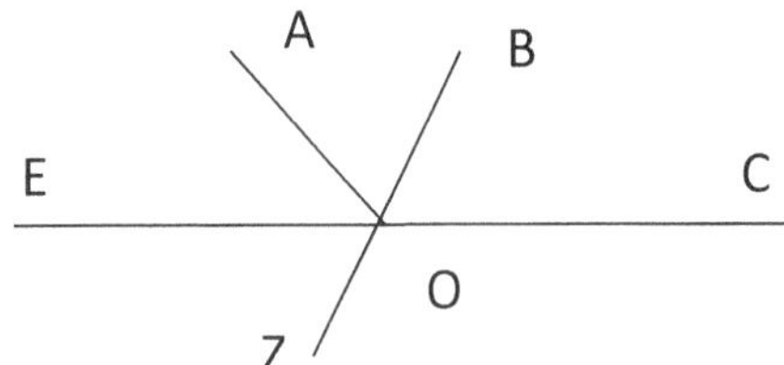

G124. A rectangular prism has a base with length 15 m, a width of 10 m, and a height of 30 m. Find the length of the diagonal that is drawn from one upper vertex to the opposite lower vertex.

G125. Find the area of an isosceles trapezoid with equal legs of 13 m, smaller base 11 m and height 12 m.

G126. The square at the right contains two squares A and B with areas 16 in^2 and 9 in^2. Region C is the remaining area of the largest square. Find the perimeter of C.

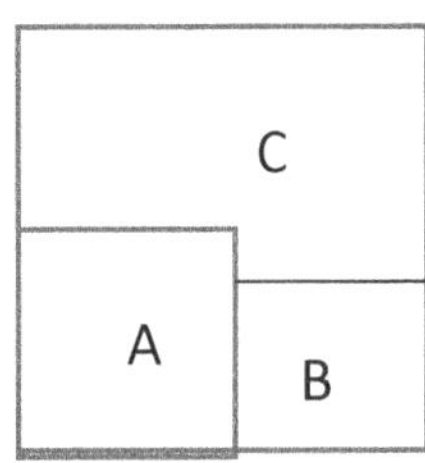

G127. Given rectangle ABCD with perimeter 54 ft. AD = BC = 10 ft. E and G are midpoints of AD and BC respectively. F lies on DC and H lies on AB. DF = BH = 5 ft. Find the area of quadrilateral EFGH.

G128. A regular square pyramid has base edge 6 m and lateral edge 5 m. Find the lateral area and total area of this pyramid.

G129. A rectangular piece of metal has an area of 35 m² and a perimeter of 24 m. What are the dimensions of this rectangular piece of metal?

G130. The sides of a rectangle are integer values with an area of 120 square units. Find the largest and smallest perimeter for this given area.

G131. Find the perimeter of
The figure at the right.
Express this perimeter
In terms of x and y.
$AB = x$, $BC = y$

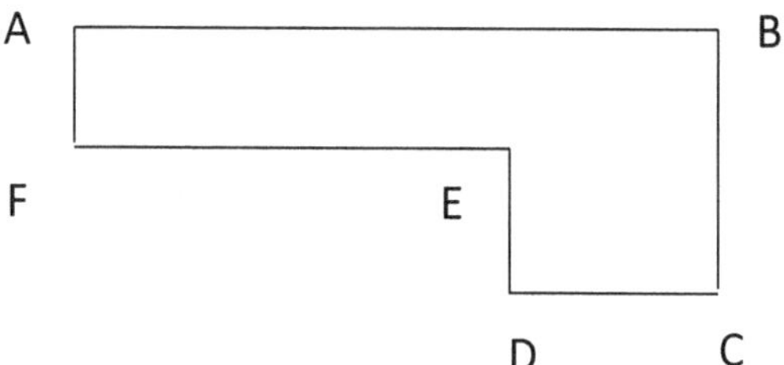

G132. In the plane figure at the right, ABCD is a square and triangle CDE is equilateral. Find the degree measure of angle CBE.

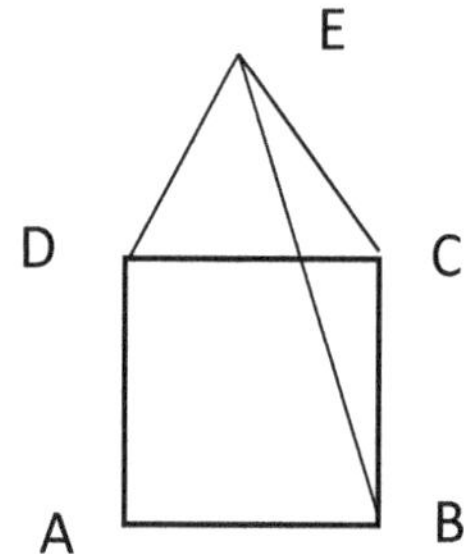

G133. At the right are two overlapping rectangles. The length of each segment of the rectangles is given in inches. Find the sum of the areas of the regions that are not overlapping.

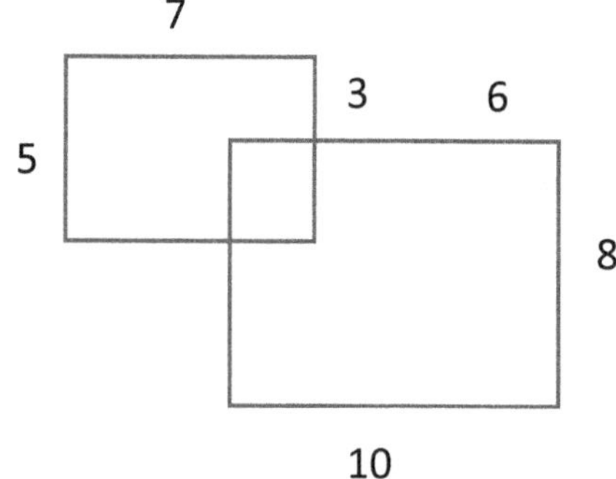

G134. A circle with radius 1 cm is inside a rectangle that is 6 cm by 10 cm. The circle rolls once around the rectangle without slipping, always touching at least one side until it returns to its starting point. Find the distance traveled by the center of the circle.

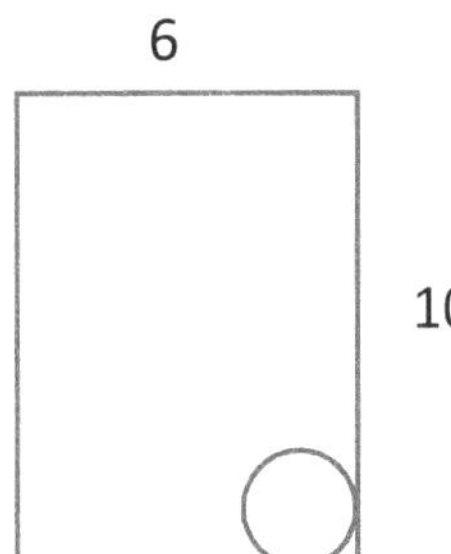

G135. Find the lateral area, total area, and volume of a rectangular prism with height 13 cm and perimeter of the base is 60 cm, and length of the base is twice the width of the base.

G136. A 25 foot ladder is leaning against a house with the foot of the ladder 7 feet from the house. If the foot of the ladder is pulled an additional 4 feet from the house, how far down the side of the house (to the nearest foot) will the ladder move?

G137. A company makes a certain cylindrical shaped bracelet pictured at the right. The height is 3 cm, the radius of the bracelet's opening is 2 cm and the bracelet material is 2 mm in width. How much material is used to make this piece of jewelry? Express the answer in terms of π.

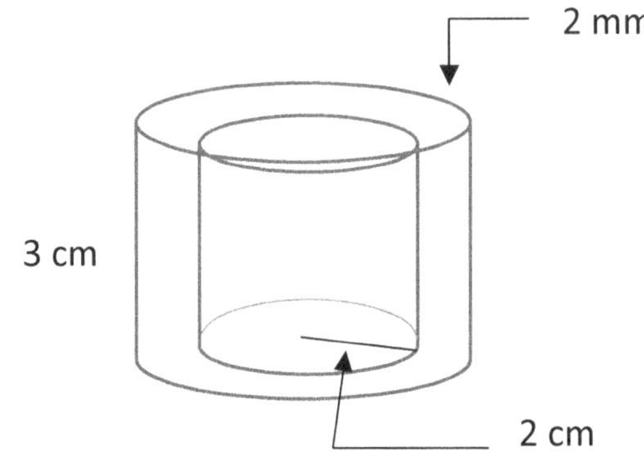

G138. The figure at the right consists of six congruent squares. The area of the figure is 96 cm^2. Find the perimeter of this figure.

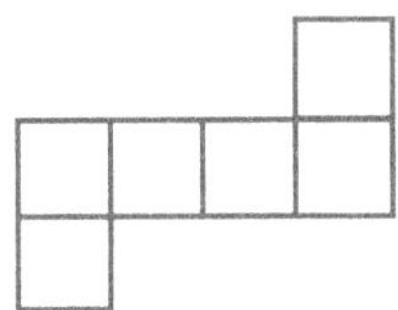

G139. A certain sprinkler releases water at the rate of 150 liters per hour. If the sprinkler operates for 80 minutes, how many liters of water will be released?

G140. Using the figures below with the given information, find the missing sides and angles.

AB = 22, $m \angle C = 90$, $m \angle B = 30$ EF = 11, $m \angle F = 90$, $EF \cong FD$

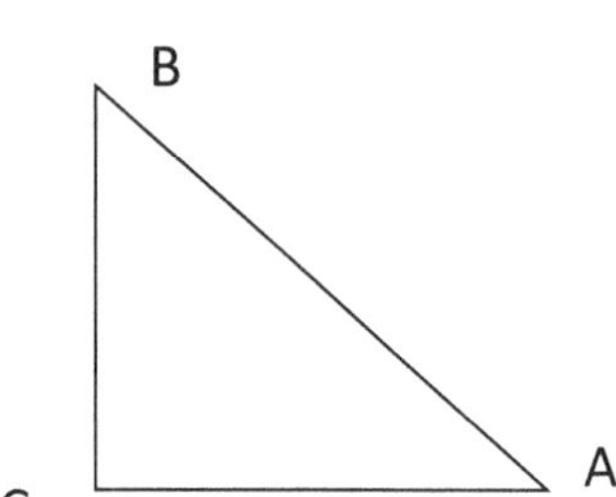 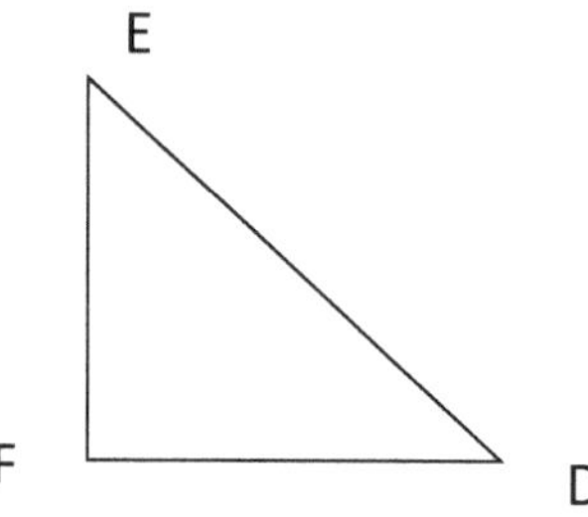

G141. If a triangle with base 8 units has the same area as a circle with radius 8 units, find the altitude of the triangle expressed as an exact value.

G142. A square pyramid has a base edge of 5 cm and a slant height of 6.5 cm. Find the total area of this figure.

G143. Two angles of a triangle measure 70° and 30°. How many degrees are in the angle formed by the bisectors of these two angles?

G144. Triangle ABC is inscribed in a circle. If $m \angle A = 73$ and the measure of the exterior angle at C is 158°, what is the measure of arc AC?

G145. If an exterior angle of a triangle equals 112° and the two opposite interior angles are of the ratio 5:2, find the other exterior angles of this triangle.

G146. Find the area of a rectangle with width 7 cm and a diagonal of length 25 cm.

G147. The supplement of an angle is three times as large as the compliment of the angle. Find the measure of the angle.

G148. The total surface area of a square prism is 1734 in². Find the volume of this prism.

G149. Find the area of an isosceles triangle with base 20 m and perimeter 72 m.

G150. The figure at the right is made up of five congruent squares. The perimeter of the figure is 72 inches. Find the area of this figure.

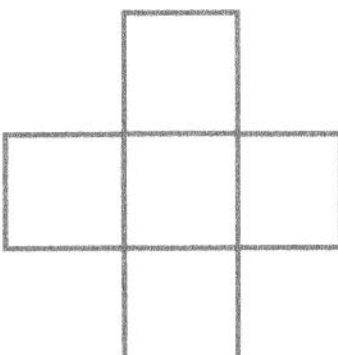

G151. An enclosed rectangular garden measures 6 yards by 15 yards. Additional fencing within the garden can divide it into three smaller plots, two of them square and one rectangular. What is the smallest amount in additional fencing needed to divide this garden?

G152. At the right is isosceles trapezoid ABCD inscribed in circle O. $\overline{AB}$ = 34 and Is a diameter of circle O. $m\overset{\frown}{AD} = m\overset{\frown}{BC} = 66$.

Find $m\overset{\frown}{DC}$, $m\angle A$, $m\angle C$

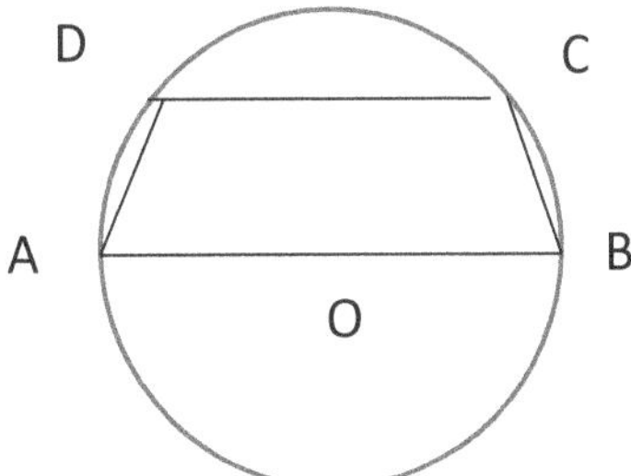

G153. A right triangular prism has base edges 5, 12, and 13 and a volume of 450. Find the height of the prism.

G154. What happens to the volume of a rectangular solid if the length and width are each doubled and the height is tripled?

G155. Find the area of a parallelogram with sides 16 ft and 20 ft that form a 30° angle.

G156. A basketball hoop is mounted on a pipe that is cemented into the ground. The hoop is 10 feet above the ground. To stop it from swaying, some students put a brace from behind the hoop to a point on the ground that is 8 feet from the cement brace. Express the length of the brace from the top of the hoop to the ground as an exact value?

G157. The sides of a rectangle are integer values with an area of 156 square units. How many different rectangles will there be that result in an area of 156 square units. Find the largest and smallest perimeter for this given area.

G158. Guido's mom is going to use 4 in square tiles to cover a rectangular floor area that is 8 feet long and 4 feet wide. How many tiles will Guido's mom need to complete this task?

G159. Joanne looked at the face of her bedroom clock when it was 3:30. She noticed that the hour hand was not exactly on the 3. She began to wonder what angle was formed by the hands of the clock at that time. Find the measure of the angle between the minute hand and the hour hand at 3:30.

G160. If each interior angle of a regular polygon has measure 150°, find the number of sides that this polygon has.

G161. All the squares in the region at the right are congruent squares. The area of the entire figure is 320 ft^2
Find the perimeter of the entire figure.

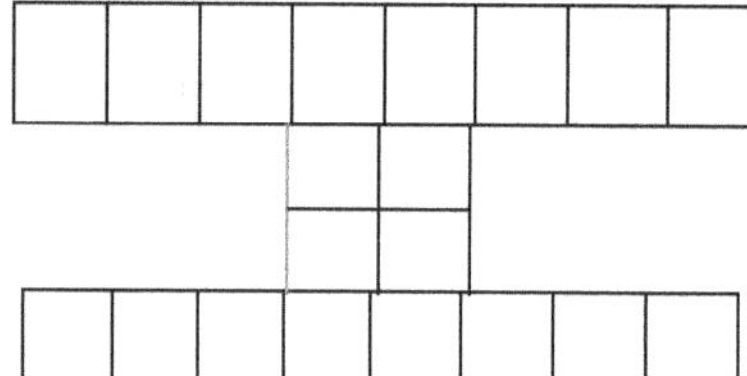

G162. In a square pyramid with base edge 16 m and slant height 10 m, find its lateral area and total area.

G163. A length of cable is 240 inches and is used to build two structures. One structure is a rectangle that is three times as long as it is wide. The second structure is a square whose side length is the same as the width of the rectangle. Find the difference in the areas of the structures.

G164. The diagonals of a rhombus are in the ratio of 1:2 and its area is 100 ft^2. Find the length of a side of this rhombus expressed as an exact value.

G165. The supplement of an angle is four times as large as the compliment of the angle. Find the measure of this angle.

G166. Two poles 25 meters and 15 meters high are cemented into the ground so that they appear in an upright position. They are attached at the top by a 14 meter long cable. Find the distance between the two poles expressed as an exact value.

G167. Two squares ABCD and AEFG with integer length sides overlap so two sides of the smaller square rest along two sides of the larger square as shown at the right. The L shaped region that is between the smaller and larger square has area 28 cm^2. Find the area of the larger square.

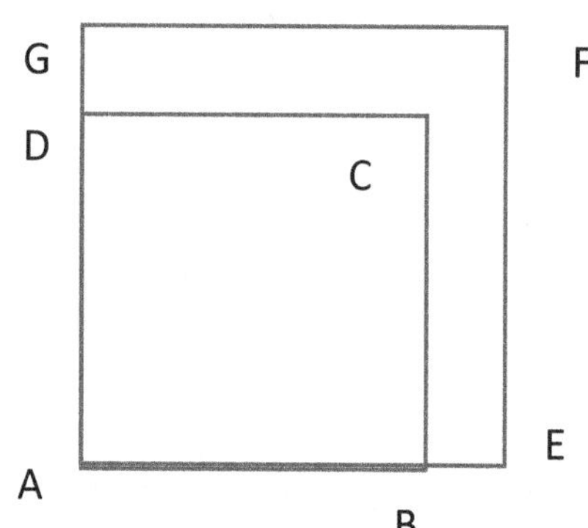

G168. (-9, 2), (-3, -12), (5, -3), and (-3, 6) are vertices of a quadrilateral. Find its area.

G169. Given right triangles BAD and BAC where C lies between A and D. DC = 19, CA = 16, DB = 37. Find the length of BC.

G170. Helen's house has 3 bedrooms. Each bedroom is 12 feet long, 10 feet wide, and 8 feet high. Helen must paint the walls of all the bedrooms. Doorways and windows which will not be painted occupy 60 ft^2 in each bedroom. How many square feet of walls must be painted?

G171. At the right is square ABCD with side 36 cm. Find the area of the region that lies outside triangle AED but inside Square ABCD.

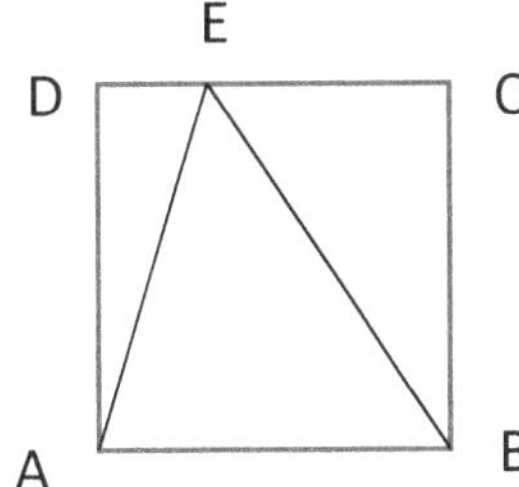

G172. If the length of a rectangle is increased by 30% and the width is decreased by 20%, what is the change in the area of the original rectangle?

G173. A rectangle with width 14 cm and diagonals of length 50 cm.

G174. Tangents to a circle from an external point are each 9 inches long and form a 60° angle. How long is the chord joining their points of tangency?

G175. A square piece of paper is folded in half to form a rectangle. The rectangle has a perimeter of 24 inches. Find the area of the original square.

G176. Using the figure at the right, the area of $\triangle ABD$ is equal to one-half the area of $\triangle ABC$. The area of $\triangle AEB$ is equal to one-third the area of $\triangle ABC$. The area of $\triangle AFB$ = 3. The area of $\triangle AFE$ = 1. Find the area of quadrilateral EFDC.

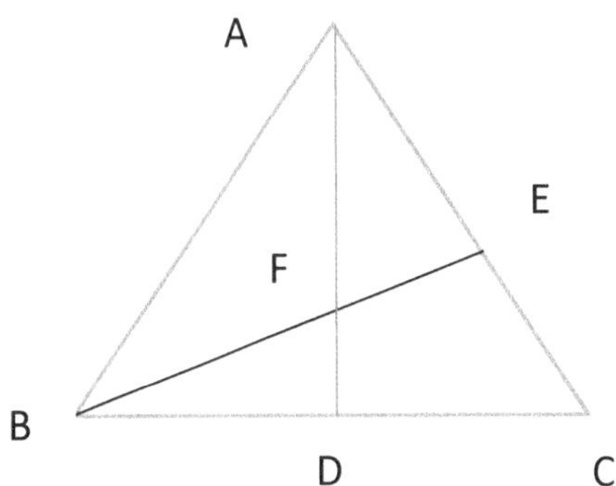

G177. The sum of the squares of the lengths of all four sides of a rectangle is 72. What is the length of the diagonal of the rectangle?

G178. A one-foot cube is to be divided completely into one-inch cubes. All of these one-inch cubes are to be placed one on top of another. How many feet high is it from the bottom of this pile of cubes to the top?

G179. The lengths of two sides of a triangle are 6 ft and 25 ft. The third side of this triangle has a length of N ft. How many whole numbers are possible values of N.

G180. Find the area of a rhombus with diagonals of length 5 m and 8 m.

G181. An altitude of a triangle is twice the base to which it is drawn. If the area of the triangle is 225 in^2, find the length of the altitude.

G182. If each interior angle of a regular polygon has measure 135˚, find the number of sides that this figure has.

G183. The area of a rectangle is 72 cm^2. The lengths of the sides are whole numbers of centimeters. What is the largest and smallest perimeter the rectangle can have?

G184. If the length of a rectangle is increased by 30% and the width is decreased by 20%, what is the change in the area of the rectangle?

G185. Find the area of an isosceles triangle with two equal sides of length 5 cm and perimeter 18 cm.

G186. Given $\triangle ABC$ inscribed in the circle.
$m\angle A = m\angle B = 50.$
Find the measure of arcs x, y, and z.

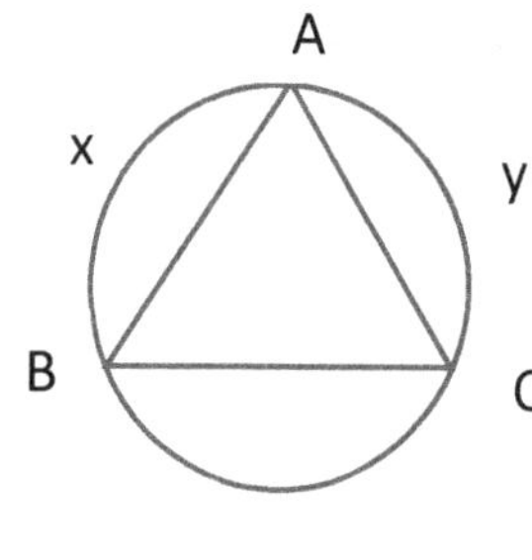

G187. A rectangular prism made of plastic has base dimensions of 30 cm by 45 cm and contains water that rises to 20 cm. When a rock is submerged, the water level rises 0.5 cm. Find the volume of the rock.

G188. Find the area of a parallelogram with sides 32 ft and 40 ft that form a $30°$ angle.

G189. Find the area of the figure at the right. AB = 26
BC = 16, DC = 10,
ED = 6, GH = 12, AH = 4

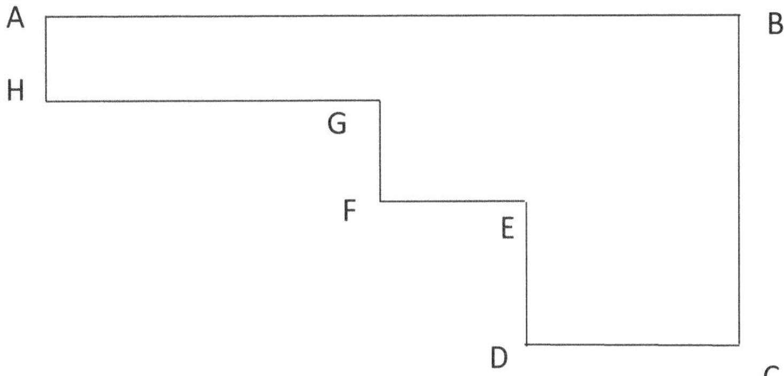

G190. The area of a square is 784 m^2. A rectangle with perimeter 120 m has a length that is three more than two times the width. Which figure is larger and by how much?

G191. A regular polygon has 13 sides. Find the sum of the measures of the interior angles of this polygon.

G192. In a right triangle, $\angle C$ is the right angle and angles A and B are the other two angles. $\overline{AB} = 78$ and $\overline{BC} = 33$. Find the missing side of the triangle expressed as an exact value.

G193. Clint is constructing two adjacent rectangular dog pens. Each pen will be three times as long as it is wide, and the pens will have a common side. If Clint has 65 feet of fencing, what are the dimensions of each pen?

G194. If a rectangle has area 72, width w, and perimeter p and if w = $\dfrac{p}{6}$, find the length l in terms of p .

G195. A rectangular solid has base dimensions of 4 inches and 6 inches and a height of 12 inches. Find the length of the solid's diagonal.

G196. If $\overrightarrow{OB}$ bisects $\angle AOC$ and $m\angle AOB$ = 5t − 7 and $m\angle AOC$ = 8t + 10 find the numerical value of $\angle BOC$.

G197. Abby is using 284 inches of wire to build two structures: (1) a rectangle that is two more than four times as long as it is wide and; (2) a square whose side length is the same as the width of the rectangle. What will be the exact area of Abby's square?

G198. Find the measure of an angle if the measures of a supplement and a compliment of the angle have the ratio 5:2.

G199. At the right is isosceles trapezoid ABCD inscribed in circle O. $\overline{AB}$ is a diameter of circle O. AB = 34. $m\widehat{AD} = m\widehat{BC} = 66$

Find: $m\widehat{DC}$, $m\angle A$, $m\angle B$, $m\angle C$

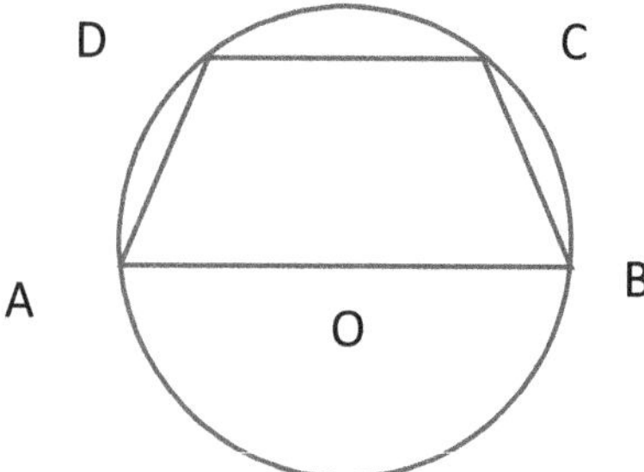

G200. Circle O has a radius of 18 cm. $\overline{OA}$ and $\overline{OB}$ are radii of circle O and $m\angle AOB = 90$. Find the length of $\overline{AB}$ as an exact value.

G201. If the length of a rectangle is increased by 30% and the width is decreased by 20%, express the change in area of the rectangle as a percent.

G202. A wire is attached from the ground 16 feet from the base of an upright utility pole to the top of the same utility pole at a point 30 feet above the ground. How long is the wire?

G203. A regular polygon has 15 sides. Find the measure of each interior angle.

G204. Juliana approaches a rectangular field on her way home from school. She knows that the sides of the field are 1000 feet and 600 feet respectively. If the field is being used, she must walk around the two sides of the field. However, if the field is not being used she can save steps by walking from one corner to the opposite corner. How many steps will she save by doing this?

G205. The rectangular base of a box has a perimeter of 4 feet. The box is $1\frac{1}{4}$ feet high and the base is three times as long as it is wide. Erin plans to cover the top and bottom with colored paper, which cost 5.5¢ per square inch. Erin then plans to cover the other four faces with white paper, which cost 2.5¢ per square inch. How much will it cost for Erin to cover the box with paper assuming that there is no waste.

G206. Two poles 25 meters and 15 meters high are cemented into the ground so that they appear in an upright position. They are attached at the top by a 14 meter long cable. Correct to hundredths, find the distance between the two poles.

G207. Three cubes with each having a volume of 8 cubic centimeters are stacked and glued together. What is the total surface area of the resulting prism?

G208. A nickel is approximately 2 mm thick and a dime is approximately 1 mm thick. Which of the following stacks has the most value: A stack of nickels 150 mm high or a stack of dimes 50 mm high?

G209. A fenced rectangular garden is 10 yards wide and 20 yards long. When one side is moved outward and the other sides are increased in length, the area increases by 40 square yards. What is the fewest number of yards of additional fencing needed to form the larger rectangular garden?

G210. A driveway 30 meters long and 5 meters wide is to be paved with blacktop 3 centimeters thick. How much will the blacktop cost if it is sold at the price of $175 per cubic meter?

G211. Find the lateral area and total area of a triangular prism with sides 24 m, 70 m, 74 m and height 13 m.

G212. Find the lateral area and total area of a square pyramid with base edge 16 m and lateral edge 17 m.

G213. If the edge of a cube is tripled, the total area is multiplied by _________ and the volume is multiplied by _________ .

G214. The length of a rectangular solid is twice the width, and the height is three times the width. If the volume is 162 cubic centimeters, find the total area of the solid.

G215. Draw a square and its inscribed and circumscribed circles. Find the ratio of the areas of these two circles.

G216. A diagonal of a cube joins two vertices not on the same face. If the diagonals are $4\sqrt{3}$ cm long, what is the volume of the cube?

G217. Nino's Pizza sells three sizes of pizza: Medium 12" for $10, Large 16" for $12 and Extra Large 19" for $15. Which size is the best buy? Show why.

G218. Find the greatest area that a rectangle can have if its perimeter is 60 feet.

G219. (-3, -4), (-2, 6), (3, 2), and (-11, 2) are vertices of a quadrilateral. Find its area.

G220. (-3, 3) and (3, 7) are points on a line. Find the equation of the line.

G221. The dimensions of a 40 foot by 25 foot rectangle are each increased by 20%. The area of the original rectangle is what percent (correct to tenths) of the new rectangle?

G222. At the right is triangle ABC. $\overline{BD}$ *bisects* $\angle B$, $\overline{CD}$ *bisects* $\angle C$, $m\angle DCB = 34$, $m\angle A = 44$. $m\angle BDC = y$, $m\angle DBC = x$. Find x and y.

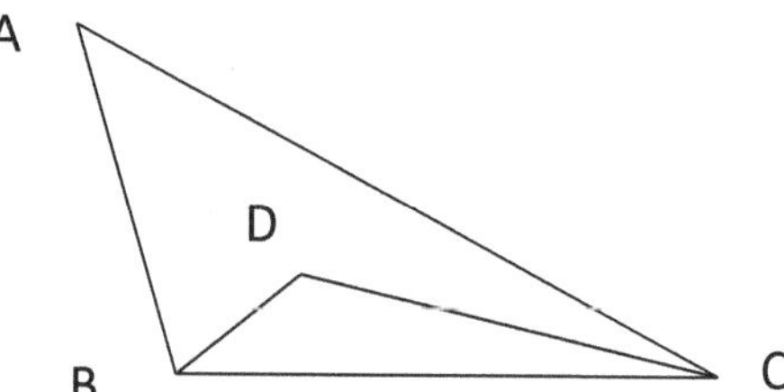

G223. A certain cereal comes in boxes 20 cm high, 4 cm wide, and 16 cm long. What is the greatest number of boxes that can fit in a carton with inside dimensions 40 cm high, 16 cm wide, and 48 cm long?

G224. The length of a rectangular solid is three times the width, and the height is twice the width. If the volume is 162 cm^3, find the total area of the solid.

G225. Find the area of an isosceles triangle with base 20 and perimeter 72.

G226. Find the area of an equilateral triangle (correct to tenths) with altitude 16.

G227. The volume of a cylinder is 225π cubic centimeters. Find the lateral area and total area of this cylinder.

G228. A clear plastic rectangular prism has base dimensions 60 cm by 90 cm and contains water that rises to 40 cm. When a rock is submerged, the water level rises 1.5 cm. Find the volume of the rock.

G229. The sides of a quadrilateral are: 6, 8, 10, and z. The corresponding sides of a similar quadrilateral are 9, x, y, and 18. Find x, y, and z.

G230. The side of the smaller, circumscribed square is 8 cm The side of the larger circumscribed square is 12 cm. Expressed as an exact value, find the area of the region that lies between the edges of the squares and the circles.

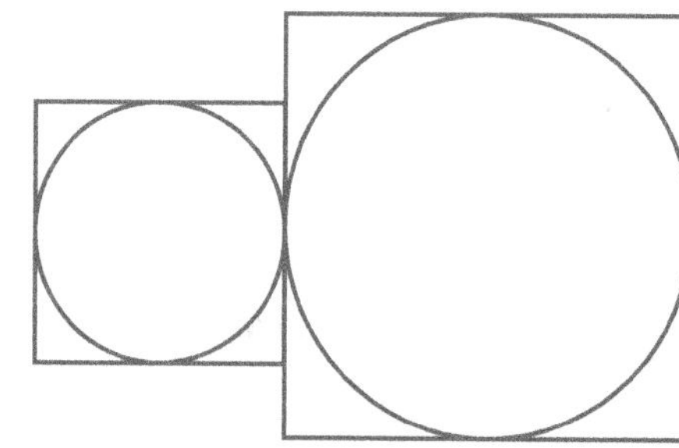

G231. A polygon has 13 sides. Find the sum of the measures of the interior angles of this polygon.

G232. Using circle O at the right, $m\widehat{AB} = 100$. $\overline{CD}$ is a diameter. $\overline{CD} \perp \overline{AB}$. $\overline{CD}$ and $\overline{AB}$ Intersect at E.

Find $m\widehat{AC}$.

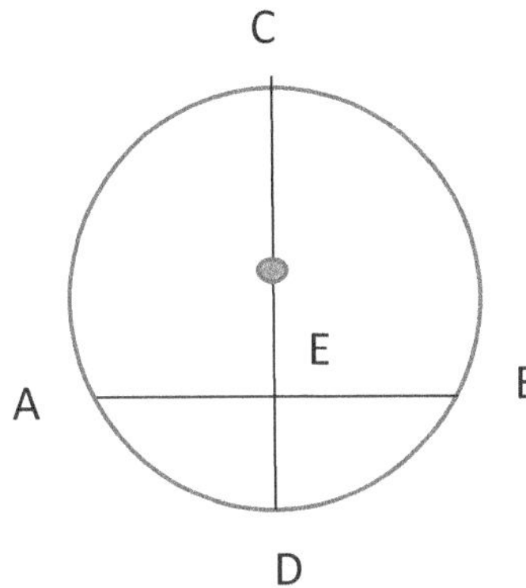

G233. Find the area of a rectangle with one side equal to 20 and inscribed in a circle with radius 26.

G234. Arrange the following plane figures from smallest to largest area: a rectangle with perimeter of 80 and the length is 1.5 times the width; a square whose side is equal to the average of the sides of the rectangle; a rhombus with side 22 and angle of 60 degrees.

G235. A metal pipe is 2 meters long and has inside radius 5 cm and outside radius 6 cm. Find the volume of the metal contained in the pipe. Express the answer in terms of π.

G236. The measures of the angles of a hexagon are in the ratio of: 5:5:5:6:7:8. Find the measures of all the angles of this hexagon.

G237. Find the area of a rhombus with a diagonal 10 meters and a side equal to 13 meters.

G238. At the right is a rectangle with dimensions 6 feet and 16 feet. What is the area of the region that lies outside triangles A and B but inside the rectangle?

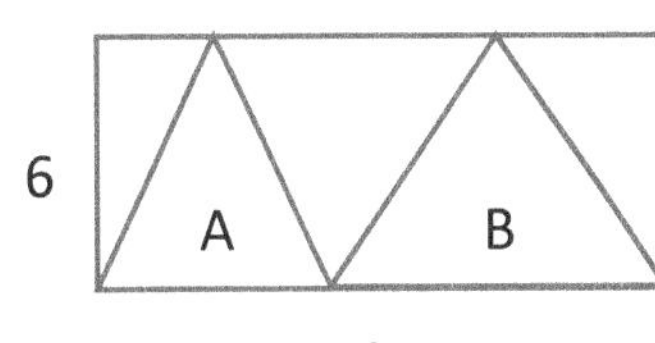

G239. A supplement of an angle is three times as large as a complement of the angle. Find the measure of the angle.

G240. Find the area of a rectangle with one side equal to 60 cm and inscribed in a circle with a radius of 34 cm.

G241. A regular polygon has 15 sides. Find the measure of each interior angle.

G242. Two angles are adjacent and form an angle that measures 120°. The larger angle is 20° less than three times the smaller angle. Find the measure of each angle.

G243. In circle O at the right, the radius is 17 cm. $\overline{AB}$ = 30 cm. Find the length of $\overline{OE}$.

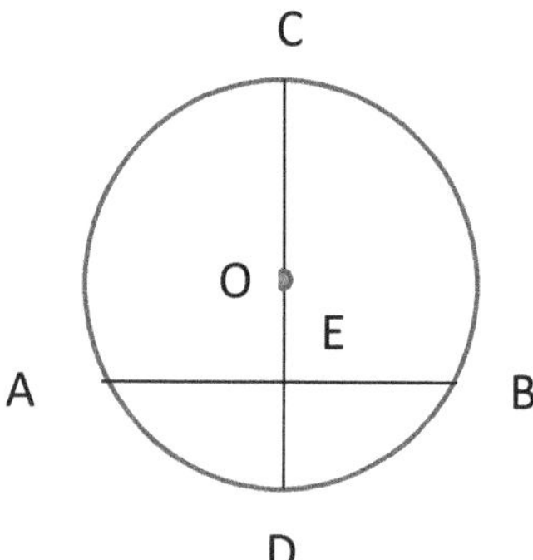

G244. The angles of a quadrilateral are in the ratio of: $3 : 4 : 5 : 6$. Find the measure of each angle.

G245. Given similar triangles LMN and PQR, $\angle L = 25$, $\angle N = 120$, NM = 3, PR = 7, $LN = 3.5$, PQ = 10. Draw the figures and find the lengths of the missing sides and measures of the missing angles.

G246. Aaron has 390 feet of fencing. After fencing in a square region, Aaron has 130 feet of fence remaining. What is the area of Aaron's square region?

G247. The angles are supplementary. One angle is 20° more than four times the other angle. Find the measure of both angles.

G248. How many cubes with 6-inch edges are required to make a cube with a volume of one cubic foot?

G249. Consider a square and its inscribed and circumscribed circles. Find the ratio of the inscribed circle to that of the circumscribed circle.

G250. Tape 2 inches wide is used to completely cover a cube 10 inches on each edge. Find the length of tape needed, if there is no overlap of the tape.

G251. Find the number of sides of a regular polygon if each exterior angle is 40°.

G252. Given rhombus ABCD. $m\angle DAB = 60$, $\overline{AD} = 20$, $\overline{AB} = 3x - 7$, $\overline{DB} = y$. Find x and y.

G253. The total area of a cylinder is 100π m^2. If the radius equals the height, find the radius, height and volume of the cylinder. Where appropriate, express answer in terms of π.

G254. How many cubes with 6-inch edges are required to make a cube one cubic foot?

G255. Using the figure at the right, find the perimeter and area of the inscribed equilateral triangle. The radius of the circle is 1 cm. Express answers as exact values.

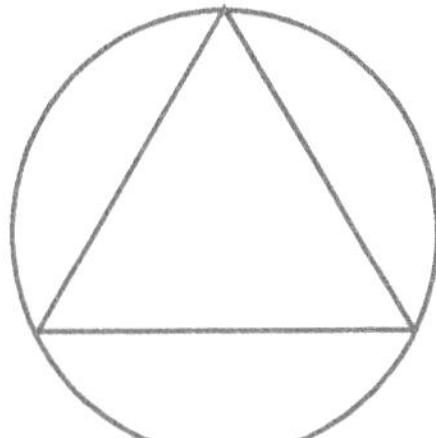

G256. A cone has a slant height of 34 ft and a radius of 16 ft. Find the volume of this cone.

G257. Given isosceles trapezoid ABCD. $m\angle DAB = 5x$, $m\angle ABC = 3x + 20$, $m\angle BCD = y$. Find x and y.

G258. Find the lateral area, total area and volume of a rectangular prism with height 13 m and perimeter of the base is 60 m. The length of the base is twice the width.

G259. A Norman window consists of a rectangular region topped by a semi-circular region. What is the area of the glass needed to fill the two regions of a Norman window whose rectangular region has width two feet and length three feet. Express you answer correct to the nearest whole number.

PROBABILITY AND STATISTICS

P001. The average of five numbers is 8. Two of the numbers are 2 and 5. The other three numbers are equal. What is the value of one of the three equal numbers?

P002. A pair of dice are tossed. What is the probability that the dice are consecutive odd numbers?

P003. A pair of dice are rolled simultaneously. What is the probability that the two numbers on the dice will result in two consecutive integers?

P004. If the average of four numbers is 37 and the average of two of these numbers is 33, what is the average of the other two numbers?

P005. Three coins are tossed. What is the probability of at least two tails?

P006. A family has 3 children. What is the probability that the children will be 2 girls and a boy?

P007. The chart at the right shows the area, in square miles, of each of the six New England states. How many New England states have an area less than the mean area of all six New England States?

State	Area
Rhode Island	1,214
Connecticut	5,009
Massachusetts	8,093
New Hampshire	9,304
Vermont	9,609
Maine	33,215

P008. A jar contains seven white marbles, two red marbles, and three blue marbles. After Joe replaces one white marble with two red marbles, Maria randomly selects a marble from the jar. What is the probability that she will select a red marble?

P009. A fair die is tossed. What is the probability that the top face shows a factor of 6?

P010. A pair of dice are tossed. What is the probability (expressed as a fraction) that the difference between the dice is two?

P011. A whole number is chosen at random from the integers 11, 12, 13, ..., 49, 50. What is the probability that the number is divisible by 3 or by 5?

P012. A bowl contains 100 pieces of colored candy: 48 green, 30 red, 12 yellow, and 10 blue. They are all wrapped in foil, so you do not know the color of any piece of candy. What is the least number of pieces you must take to be sure that you have at least 15 pieces of the same color?

P013. The mean, the median, and the mode of the set of numbers {1.8, 1.6, 2.1, 1.7, N} are all equal. What number does N represent?

P014. In Helen's history class, the only grades that count towards the semester average are the 6 tests she has already taken and the upcoming final exam. The final exam counts as two tests. She has determined that if she earns 99 points on the final exam, she will have a 90 point average for the semester. On average, how many points has Helen scored on each test prior to the final exam?

P015. Each of the four test scores in Connie's class is to be weighted equally. Connie scores 79, 87 and 98 on the first three tests. What grade must she score on her fourth test to have an overall average of exactly 90.

P016. A pair of standard dice are tossed. What is the probability that the product of the two numbers showing on the dice are divisible by 3?

P017. If three coins are tossed, what is the probability of at least two heads?

P018. A bag contains 200 discs numbered 1 through 200. What is the probability of selecting a disc that is neither the square or cube of a positive integer?

P019. A tetrahedron (with faces numbered 1 through 4) and an octahedron (with faces numbered 1 through 8) are tossed. What is the probability that the sum of the "up" faces of the tetrahedron and the "up" face of the octahedron is a multiple of 5.

P020. A set of 5 different positive integers has a mean 0f 33 and a median of 40. Within this set, how large can the greatest integer be?

P021. What is the probability of showing consecutive integers when tossing a pair of dice?

P022. A die and two coins are tossed. What is the probability that the outcome will be a 3 and two heads?

P023. Taylor has a set of blocks of which five are square, six are round, and four are triangular. She randomly picks a block and sets it aside. The she randomly picks another block. What is the probability that both blocks are square?

P024. Kim rolls a tetrahedron numbered 1 to 4 and Jim rolls a standard 6 sided die numbered 1 to 6. What is the probability that Kim's face down number is greater than Jim's face up number?

P025. In a dice game, a player loses if a two, three, or twelve occurs on the first roll. What is the probability of losing on the first roll?

P026. A cube with faces numbered 1 to 6 and an octahedron with faces number 1 to 8 are tossed. What is the probability of the up face of each solid shows a sum of 11.

P027. A circle with a diameter of 10 feet is inscribed in a square. What is the probability that a thrown dart will land outside the circle but inside the square. Express the answer as an exact value.

P028. What is the probability of getting a prime number if a tetrahedron with its "up" faces (the faces of a tetrahedron are numbered from 1 to 4) and a die with its "up "face (faces of a die are number 1 to 6) are tossed?

P029. Find the average of the largest 3 digit perfect square and largest 3 digit perfect cube.

P030. A family has 4 children. What is the probability that the children will be 2 girls and two boys?

P031. A tetrahedron (with faces numbered 1 through 4) and an octahedron (with faces numbered 1 through 8) are tossed. What is the probability that the sum of the "up" faces of the tetrahedron and the "up" face of the octahedron is a prime number?

P032. A dart board is constructed with a right triangle having sides 12, 16 and 20 inscribed in a circle. If a dart is tossed at this figure, what is the probability that it will land outside the triangle but inside the circle?   Express the answer as an exact value.

P033. A tetrahedron (with faces numbered 1 through 4) and an octahedron (with faces numbered 1 through 8) are tossed. What is the probability that the product of the "up" faces of the tetrahedron and the "up" face of the octahedron is a multiple of 6.

P034. If the average of eight consecutive integers arranged in increasing order is 15.5, what is the average of the first three of these integers?

P035. On the first three tests, Hanley had an average of 76. On the next two tests, he had an average of 81. What is his average for the five tests?

P036. A family has 3 children. What is the probability that the children will be 3 girls and a boy?

P037. Grandma's cookie jar has 6 peanut butter cookies, twice as many chocolate chip cookies, and one more oatmeal cookie than chocolate chip cookies. Your person favorite is peanut butter so what are the chances of pulling out your favorite from the cookie jar?

P038. If the average of four numbers is 53 and the average of two of these numbers is 41, what is the average of the other two numbers?

P039. Randi's five test scores have a mean of 69. The median is 83 and the mode is 85. If the range of the five scores is 70, find the value of the second lowest test score.

P040. What is the average of the of the sum of the first 10,000 positive integers.

P041. Jane was sick so she had to make up an exam a few days after her class took the exam. Without her exam score, the class average was 71. After she took the exam, the class average was 72. If her grade was 96%, how many students were in the class?

P042. If $2 \leq y \leq 3$ and $4 \leq z \leq 5$, then the least possible average of $\dfrac{1}{y}$ and $\dfrac{1}{z}$ is:

P043. The average of five numbers is 25. Four of the numbers are 19, 21, 24, and 25. Find the other number.

P044. The mean annual salary for 16 employees of a company in Groton is $38,250. If one employee receives a $2,500 raise and another receives a $3,500 raise, how will the mean salary of all 16 employees be affected?

P045. Anna receives a set of 4 grades on her math tests. If the average of her first two grades is 50, the average of the second and third is 75 and the average of the third and fourth is 70, then what is the average of the first and fourth?

P046. What integer n could be included in the set of integers $\{6, 11, 13, 7, 14\}$ so that the mean is equal to n+1.

P047. You roll an octahedron and a tetrahedron. Using the faces of these two polyhedrons that are on the plane surface, what is the probability of rolling a prime number?

P048. You have a spinner with 8 equal sectors numbered 1 to 8 and a six-sided die numbered 1 to 6. The spinner is spun once, and the die is tossed once. What is the probability that the sum of the numbers on these two objects is 10?

P049. A family has 4 children. What is the probability that the children will be at least one girls and 3 boys?

P050. A bag contains some marbles, all of the same size. Eight of them are yellow. The rest of the marbles are blue. The probability of drawing a blue marble from the bag is $\dfrac{2}{3}$. Find the total number of blue marbles in the bag.

P051. A jar contains 8 white marbles, 3 red marbles, and 4 blue marbles. One white marble is replaced by two red marbles, one red marble is replaced by two blue marbles, one blue marble is replaced by two white marbles. One marble is drawn from the jar. What is the probability that it is red?

P052. A gumball machine contains red, green, yellow, and purple gumballs. You cannot choose which color you get. Janet wants 3 gumballs of the same color. At 5¢ each, what is the most Janet must spend to be sure that she has three gumballs of the same color?

P053. A square is inscribed in a circle of diameter 12 feet. What is the probability (correct to hundredths) of a thrown dart landing in the area outside the square but inside the circle. Use $\pi = 3.14$.

P054. Ten families have an average of 2 children per family. If exactly 2 of these families are childless, what is the average number of children (correct to tenths) in the families with children?

P055. The mean of the following numbers: x, $(2x - 4)$, $(4x - 3)$, -13, 9, $(5x + 2)$, $(x - 2)$ is 4. Find the median and mode for these numbers.

P056. A circle with a diameter of 10 feet is inscribed in a square. What is the probability (expressed as an exact value) that a thrown dart will land outside the circle but inside the square?

P057. If the average of four numbers is 53 and the average of two of these numbers is 41, what is the average of the other two numbers?

P058. A rectangle with length 16 and width 12 is inscribed in a circle. Find the probability of tossing a dart that lands inside the circle but outside the rectangle. Express the answer as an exact value.

P059. Tickets numbered 1 to 20 are mixed and drawn at random. What is the probability of drawing a number that is a multiple of 3 or 5?

P060. A die is tossed, and a coin is flipped. What is the probability that the face of the die is odd number, and the coin is a head?

P061. A die with faces labeled A through F and a tetrahedron with faces labeled A through D are tossed. With the tetrahedron's down face and the die's up face, what is the probability of both faces showing a vowel?

P062. A die with faces labeled A through F and a tetrahedron with faces labeled A through D are tossed. With the tetrahedron's down face and the die's up face, what is the probability of both faces showing the same letter?

P063. A die with faces labeled A through F and a tetrahedron with faces labeled A through D are tossed. With the tetrahedron's down face and the die's up face, what is the probability of both faces showing consecutive letters?

P064. If $6 \le y \le 7$ and $3 \le z \le 4$, find the largest possible average of $\dfrac{1}{y}$ and $\dfrac{1}{z}$.

P065. Becca scored 10, 15, 20, 15, 10, 20, 20, 20 in her first 8 basketball games. How many points would she need to score in the ninth game so that the mean, median, and mode of her 9 point totals have the same value?

P066. A die is tossed twice. What is the probability that the sum of the faces of the die is 9?

P067. The average of a set of 10 numbers is 15. If one of the numbers is removed from the set, the average of the remaining numbers is 14. What is the value of the number that was removed?

P068. A pair of dice are rolled. What is the probability of rolling a composite number.

ALGEBRA ANSWERS

A001. $1.29 & $0.87

A002. 2x + 3

A003. 3 days

A00. $-4y^3 + y^2 - 13y + 21$

A005. 0

A006. $\dfrac{13}{3}$

A007. $145

A008. 220 km

A009. $\dfrac{1}{100}$

A010. 3x − 4y = −24

A011. −1

A012. 1

A013. 10 hrs

A014. $\dfrac{9}{23}$

A015. x < 0

A016. 36 mph

A017 10,000,001

A018. 2

A019. 7, 12

A020. 2x − 3y = −9

A021. $2

A022. $12x^2 - 5x - 2 = 0$

A023. 2

A024. 10.6 miles

A025. 11

A026. 12

A027. 0

A028. 5

A029. $C = \dfrac{3}{5}P - 3$

A030. 2

A031. 9

A032. $-\dfrac{2y^2}{(x+y)(x-y)}$

A033. $200

A034. 5

A035. $\dfrac{2}{5}$, $\dfrac{1}{3}$

A036. 238

A037. $-\dfrac{3}{4}$

A038. y^2

A039. 7 & 11

A040. At least 16 problems

A041. 29

A042. $\dfrac{7}{3}$

A043. 4

A044. 5:30

A045. 17 minutes

A046. 240 km

A047. 7

A048. (11 − 3.50 − 0.75)N

A049. $13

A050. 12.4 ft

A051. 3 PM

A052. $9a^3 - 9a^2 + 11a - 3$

A053. $\dfrac{16}{13}$

A054. $10k^3$

A055. 9x

A056. 0.005

A057. 50

A058. 37

A059. 2, −4

A060. $\dfrac{1}{3}$

A061. 6, −3

A062. $X^2 + 5x + 6$

A063. $2\sqrt{34}$

A064. 4 hrs

A065. 41

A066. 1

A067. 1 hr, 22 min

A068. $14

A069. 66

A070. 0 < x < 0.5

A071. 5

A072. 128 lbs

A073. 2, −2

A074. 500

A075. $\dfrac{k^2}{3}$

A076. 15

A077. 4:30 PM

A078. $32.99

A079. 1

A080. 54

A081. 32

A082. 16, 27

A083. (4, 3)

A084. 17

A085. U = 10, B = 40, T = 20

A086. $\dfrac{16}{13}$

A087. 1

A088. 2

A089. 14 mph

A090. 12

A091. 1

A092. X(6x + 1)(x + 4)

A093. d = 9, n = 27

A094. $\left(\dfrac{1}{4},\ 1\right)$

A095. $5\dfrac{1}{2}$

A096. 2182

A097. 20¢

A098. 14

A099. 0.5

A100. $(x − 2)^2(x + 2)$

A101. 0, 3

A102. $\dfrac{189}{199}$

A103. (−6, −1)

A104. 22.5

A105. $\dfrac{28}{47}$

A106. 129, 131, 133

A107. 16 mph

A108. X = m + 10

A109. (4, −9)

A110. 528

A111. $\dfrac{1}{3}a^2 − 2a + 5$

A112. $\dfrac{a}{2n − p}$

A113. y = x^2 − 4x − 12

A114. 0

A115. y = −x + 1

A116. 6

A117. 16

A118. 42

A119. (3, 4), (7, 1)

A120. x^2 + x + 1

A121. $15

A122. More than 50 miles

A123. $\dfrac{a + b}{2}$

A124. $\dfrac{2A}{h} − b$

A125. 625

A126. $1.00

A127. $-\dfrac{27}{2}$

A128. 7

A129. 1

A130. (5, −4)

A131. $-\dfrac{4}{15}$

A132. $\sqrt{6}$

A133. $\dfrac{5}{27}$

A134. H = 11, D = 15, L = 17

A135. 32m

A136. 54

A137. 42

A138. A = 7, B = 5

A139. D = 14, Q = 4

A140. 45

A141. (−4, 5) and (3, 12)

A142. 10

A143. Curly, 9

A144. $\dfrac{15}{19}$

A145. $\dfrac{1}{12}$

A146. 8 ft

A147. 5

A148. 144

A149. 20

A150. 20

A151. 39

A152. $6,000

A153. 12

A154. 1

A155. 5

A156. 15

A157. M =18, W = 27

A158. 14

A159. 28

A160. $\dfrac{3}{4}$

A161. −108

A162. $x > -\dfrac{21}{2}$

A163. $x \ge \dfrac{22}{5}$

A164. $-\dfrac{47}{16}$

A165. 104 km

A166. $75.45

A167. 39

A168. 1

A169. $36

A170. 120

A171. 380

A172. $-\dfrac{21}{4}$

A173. $\dfrac{2}{7}$

A174. P = 16z

A175. 120

A176. 8 mph

A177. 1, −4

A178. $\dfrac{11}{18}$

A179. $\left(-1, \dfrac{1}{77}\right)$

A180. 37.2 mph

A181. 2

A182. write more than 80 check

A183. $\dfrac{23}{86}$

A184. $\dfrac{2A}{5A-4}$

A185. −13

A186. 15

A187. 18, 30, 55

A188. $\dfrac{1}{4}$

A189. Y = x² + 2x − 24

A190. 14

A191. 2, 4

A192. 2, −6

A193. 4, 6

A194. $16

A195. 16

A196. 12

A197. (3,0), (7,0), (0,21), (5,−4)

A198. 7, −3

A199. (−6,0), (4,0), (0,−24), (−1,−25)

A200. (−7,0), (−5,0), (0,35), (−6,−1)

A201. $\dfrac{5}{3}, -1$

A202. (x + 7)(x − 2)

A203. $\dfrac{7}{12}$

A204. $\dfrac{a}{2n-p}$

A205. $\dfrac{8}{9}$

A206. −1

A207. 16

A208. $\dfrac{3F}{h} - \dfrac{b}{2}$

A209. (0,9), (−9,0), (−3,0), (1,0), (0,−3)

A210. (−4,5) and (3,12)

A211. 3.72 seconds

A212. 78

A213. 70

A214. 3, 7, −2

A215. All reals, x ≠ ±1

A216. −5, −8

A217. $-\dfrac{11}{5}$

A218. 8,160

A219. East 171 miles, West 147 miles

A220. $\dfrac{8}{9}$

A221. X(6x + 1)(x + 4)

A222. $y = \dfrac{2}{3}x + 5$

A223. 23

A224. $\dfrac{7}{12}$

A225. f: (0,9), (−9,0). g: (−3,0), (1,0), (0,−3). (−4,0) & (3,0)

A226. $C = \dfrac{2A}{H} - B$

A227. 48

A228. 9a³ − 9a² + 11a − 3

A229. 13

A230. $\dfrac{23}{86}$

A231. 4

A232. 240 m

A233. $\dfrac{28}{5}$

A234. $y = -\dfrac{2}{3}x + 5$

A235. 32

NUMBER THEORY ANSWERS

N001. $\dfrac{17}{6}$

N002. −73

N003. 45 and 54

N004. 33

N005. 6

N006. 8

N007. 5

N008. +

N009. 6

N010. $15,000

N011. 21

N012. $\dfrac{9}{44}, \dfrac{5}{22}, \dfrac{1}{4}$

N013. −2

N014. 47

N015. 45 sec < time < 72 sec

N016. 241

N017. 183

N018. 24

N019. 3446

N020. 909

N021. 17,964

N022. 8

N023. 99

N024. 17

N025. 43, 47

N026. 120 min

N027. 33

N028. 7

N029. $\dfrac{55}{126}$

N030. 36

N031. 10

N032. 64

N033. 12

N034. 9

N035. 28 and 82

N036. 1041_5

N037. 29

N038. 60

N039. A=3, B=7, C=6, D=5

N040. 246

N041. 60

N042. $\dfrac{8}{15}$

N043. Moe

N044. {1, 5, 7, 11, 13, 17, 18}

N045. $18\sqrt{5} - 5\sqrt{3}$

N046. 16

N047. $\dfrac{25n}{18}$

N048. 36

N049. $\dfrac{306}{25}$

N050. 57

N051. GCF=18, LCM=106,812

N052. 55

N053. 3

N054. 1926

N055. $13

N056. 205

N057. $\dfrac{1}{1064}$

N058. 44

N059. 57

N060. 135

N061. 1 PM

N062. 31

N063. 1065

N064. 197

N065. $55,686.47

N066. 25¢

N067. 7

N068. 27

N069. 68

N070. 20

N071. 7

N072. 9

N073. 160

N074. 3:06 PM

N075. 235

N076. 72

N077. 3, 9, 27, 81

N078. 22

N079. 357 and 49,980

N080. $\dfrac{1}{4}$

N081. 0.0625%

N082. D^E

N083. 625

N084. $\dfrac{14}{21}$

N085. 4

N086. 4985.01

N087. 60

N088. $\dfrac{4}{n^8}$

N089. 49

N090. 2:46 PM

N091. 8

N092. 9

N093. 3

N094. 70

N095. 200

N096. 12

N097. 8

N098. $\dfrac{26}{99}$

N099. D, 50

N100. $\dfrac{1}{4}$

N101. 8

N102. 13, $1\dfrac{1}{4} inches$

N103. 12

N104. 37

N105. 315

N106. $2\dfrac{3}{11}m$

N107. 13¢

N108. 19

N109. 145

N110. 270 miles

N111. 4

N112. 720

N113. Family @ 23¢/oz

N114. $\dfrac{2}{3}$

N115. 78

N116. 7945

N117. 21

N118. 21

N119. 95¢

N120. 95%

N121. 45

N122. $\dfrac{16807}{2048}$

N123. 450

N124. 3

N125. 9

N126. 18

N127. 4

N128. 82,656

N129. $\dfrac{2}{99}$

N130. 50

N131. 2,056

N132. {20}, {8, 14, 20, 26}

N133. 1089

N134. $a = \dfrac{1}{6}c$

N135. 30

N136. 595

N137. 29

N138. $\dfrac{23}{36}$

N139. 23

N140. 6, 17, 58

N141. 11

N142. 357

N143. 30

N144. 12

N145. $-\dfrac{47}{16}, -\dfrac{21}{4}$

N146. A = 2, B = 1

N147. 16, $1\dfrac{1}{3}$ *inches of wire wasted*

N148. 28

N149. 39

N150 $99,000

N151. 78

N152. 6754

N153. 57

N154. 1,999,999,999,997

N155. 13

N156. −988

N157. 180

N158. $77\dfrac{7}{9}$

N159. $\dfrac{5}{6}$

N160. 40%

N161. 84

N162. $\dfrac{1}{1000}$

N163. 17

N164. 39

N165. 0.1%

N166. fifth

N167. $\dfrac{2}{5}$

N168. 34

N169. 1,024

N170. 15 mph

N171. 312,132 or 231,213

N172. 315, 630, 945, 1260, 1575

N173. 9600 gallons

N174. 1, 2, 4

N175. 444

N176. 199%

N177. 13

N178. 96

N179. 23

N180. 112 cups

N181. 13.7%

N182. $\dfrac{11}{18}$

N183. 1, 3, 5, 7, 9

N184. 5,625

N185. 275

N186. 16

N187. 1, 4, 7

N188. 18

N189. $150

N190. 53

N191. 21

N192. $\dfrac{243}{17}$

N193. 1

N194. 4, 9, 25, 49

N195. $\dfrac{243}{170}$

N196. $\dfrac{a^{27}}{b^{14}}$

N197. 12453

N198. $\dfrac{8}{15}$

N199. $9.60

N200. 100,500

N201. 30 digits

N202. 24

N203. $\dfrac{27}{13}$

N204. $\dfrac{3a-4}{1-10a-5a^2}$

N205. 3

N206. $\dfrac{20}{3}$

N207. 12

N208. 30 seconds

N209. 6

N210. 599

N211. 123

N212. 88

N213. $\dfrac{3}{7}$

N214. 36

N215. 7

N216. GCF = 132, LCM = 113,256

N217. 26

N218. 1, p, p^2, p^3, t pt, p^{2}t, p^{3}t

N219. 8,888

N220. 1, 2, 4, 7, 14, 28

N221. 2

N222. 45

N223. 20, 8

N224. 39

N225. 5

N226. $\dfrac{19}{110}$

N227. 87

N228. 310

N229. 305

N230. 6

N231. 91¢

N232. 33

N233. 3998

N234. R=24, W=36, B=48

N235. $\dfrac{64}{27}$

N236. 5040

N237. 6

N238. 13

N239. $\dfrac{1}{50}$

N240. K: 9AM, L: 11AM, J: 1 PM

N241. 156

N242. 58

N243. 867

N244. 1, 3, 5, 7, 9

N245. 4

N246. 32, 48, 56

N247. 1 minute, 49 seconds

N248. $123 + 45 - 67 + 8 - 9 = 100$

N249. 21,387

N250. 3, 7

N251. 30

N252. 1

N253. 2 feet, 9 inches

N254. 84

N255. 53

N256. 28 lbs

N257. 8

N258. 7,317

N259. 196

N260. ÷3: R=1, ÷9: R=4, ÷11: R=6

N261. $\dfrac{28}{99}$, Ted, Frank, Gary

N262. 144

N263. 80

N264. 204

N265. $\dfrac{16}{13}$

N266. 5, x = 6

N267. $\dfrac{40}{51}$

N268. $\dfrac{24}{7}$

N269. 756

N270. 7 mph

N271. 8

N272. $-\dfrac{1}{12}$

N273. a=1 & b=12, c=9 & d=10

N274. 5,839

N275. 3, 7

N276. n = 2x + 6

N277. 8

N278. 35

N279. 6

N280. 24, 36, 52

N281. 25 & 27, −27 & −25

N282. 1112, 111, 10011101

N283. $\dfrac{98}{225}$

N284. 7

N285. 0, 6

N286. 2 17

N287. 2

N288. $\dfrac{135}{4802}$

N289. 8

N290. 101

N291. 23

N292. 10

N293. $2.00

N294. $\dfrac{63}{17}$

N295. 10

N296. $\dfrac{479}{660}$

N297. $\dfrac{5}{8}$

N298. 10,599

N299. 5

N300. 81,600

N301. 9

N302. 32

N303. 4

N304. 10001111

N305. 3956

N306. 135,450

N307. 9

N308. $\dfrac{5}{9}$

N309. 5

N310. 6

N311. $\dfrac{1}{5}$

N312. 10

N313. $\dfrac{8}{11}$

N314. −2320

N315. −2

N316. 40,000

N317. 70m

N318. 141

N319. 11

N320. 15 rides

N321. {a,b,c}, {a,b,d}, {a,c,d}, {b,c,d}

N322. 6

N323. 62

N324. MMMCDXCIV

N325. 4,950

N326. 8:57 AM

N327. 210

N328. 5

N329. 9

N330. 0, 4, 8

N331. 4

N332. 95

N333. 2,149

N334. $18\sqrt{5}-5\sqrt{3}$

N335. 1, 2, 7, 14

N336. MMCMXLIV

N337. −920

N338. $\dfrac{8}{15}$

N339. 15

N340. 10001010

N341. 18

N342. x = 6, y = 4

N343. 8

N344. 90,300

N345. $\dfrac{10}{9}$

N346. 50¢

N347. 1,360 cases

N348. 3+7+13; 5+7+11

N349. 30

N350. $\dfrac{1}{25}$

N351. 5

N352. 2520

N353. 301

N354. 2

N355. 128

N356. 259

N357. 120

N358. $2,100

N359. 900

N360. Don

N361. $\dfrac{2}{15}$

N362. 30

N363. 8

N364. 20

N365. $18,444

N366. $\dfrac{8}{15}$

N367. $25,900

N368. 8640

N369. $\dfrac{24}{25}$

N370. $\dfrac{91}{330}$

N371. 61,425

N372. 3

N373. 4985.01

N374. D

N375. 0.16%

N376. $\dfrac{23}{80}$

N377. 20

N378. 25

N379. x = 15,625, y = 7

N380. 1:15 PM

N381. $291.60

N382. 3998

N383. $\dfrac{11}{160}$

N384. $\dfrac{324}{7}$

N385. $\dfrac{625}{192}$

N386. 275%

N387. $\dfrac{8}{15}, \dfrac{9}{16}, \dfrac{7}{12}, \dfrac{5}{8}$

N388. $1,600

N389. A

N390. 5

N391. Item B

N392. 60

N393. 3.4

N394. 1

N395. $50,000

N396. 32

N397. 121

N398. 143

N399. $24,800

N400. $3,200

N401. $23,450

N402. 61

N403. 86

N404. 125

N405. 0.01%

N406. $-\dfrac{16}{55}$

N407. 43.75%

N408. 105, 14

N409. $\dfrac{3025}{768}$

N410. 122

N411. 121

N412. $-\dfrac{22}{9}$

N413. $a^5 b^{11} c^5$

N414. −11

N415. 3780, 5040, 6300, . . .

N416. L:G:R = 33:28:11

N417. 1, 2, 4, 7, 14, 28

N418. $\dfrac{41}{111}$

N419. 400

N420. 17

N421. $\dfrac{3}{1024}$

N422. 5

N423. 10

N424. $\dfrac{40}{51}$

N425. $\dfrac{21}{13}$

N426. $6\sqrt{3}$

N427. $18,445.16

N428. 6 weeks

N429. 15:14

N430. 2

N431. $\dfrac{479}{660}$

N432. 1,682

N433. 3

N434. 32

N435. $\dfrac{3}{7}$

N436. 0, 6

N437. 60

N438. 2

N439. $\dfrac{135}{4802}$

N440. $\dfrac{479}{660}$

N441. 756

N442. 4994.99

N443. 30

N444. 52%

N445. 360

N446. $\dfrac{77}{111}$

N447. 20

N448. 6

N449. 18, 24, 42

N450. 1000

N451. $\dfrac{1}{6}$, three possibilities: $\dfrac{25}{168}, \dfrac{26}{168}, \dfrac{27}{168}$

N452. 13

N453. $\dfrac{19}{110}$

N454. 1, 3, 5, 7, 9

N455. Any fraction > $\dfrac{9}{40}$, i.e. $\dfrac{19}{80}$

N456. 2:40 PM

N457. 1512 chicken

N458. 8,352

N459. 20

N460. 6

N461. $\dfrac{12}{11}$

N462. 288

N463. 40,000

N464. 50

N465. $19,440

N466. 5 times

N467. 12

N468. 79

N469. $\dfrac{2n^2}{15m}$

N470. 20, 30, 48

N471. 250,500

N472. 2, 8

N473. −11

N474. 12

GEOMETRY AND MEASUREMENT ANSWERS

G001. 56.25

G002. 540 cm^2

G003. D, B, A, C

G004. $7 + 2\sqrt{2}$

G005. 1089 cm^2

G006. 5

G007. 10 ft^2

G008. 17 in

G009. 12π

G010. 5625 ft^2

G011. $\dfrac{d^2}{2}$

G012. 377 inches

G013. 120°

G014. (x − 2)

G015. $4\pi - 3\sqrt{3}\,cm^2$

G016. 96 cm^2

G017. 62, 118

G018. 42 sq units

G019. 2.5 km

G020. 30.4 in

G021. 1500 cm^3

G022. $\dfrac{x}{4}$

G023. $48\sqrt{3}\,cm^2$

G024. 8

G025. $\dfrac{2}{\pi\sqrt{\pi}}$

G026. $64 - 16\pi$ cm^2

G027. 144 m^2

G028. $42 + 2\sqrt{41}$

G029. 126 cm

G030. 90°

G031. 2160

G032. 100 ft X 100 ft

G033. 441x^2

G034. 11

G035. $36\sqrt{3}\,cm^2$

G036. 3 liters

G037. 36 cm^2

G038. 400 cm^2

G039. 80 cm^2

G040. 3

G041. 12

G042. 260 yds

G043. 15

G044. 1,440,000 in^3

G045. 24

G046. 156, 24

G047. x=2, y=8

G048. 34°

G049. 26

G050. 48π

G051. 30 ft

G052. 5 ft

G053. 54 ft

G054. 46 cm

G055. 1,250

G056. 38

G057. 7π cm^2

G058. 30

G059. $\dfrac{1}{2}$

G060. D

G061. 3 cm

G062. 6

G063. 1692

G064. 14

G065. 40%

G066. 12 cm, 24 cm, 30 cm

G067. 7,333.3 ft

G068. 240 cm^2

G069. LA=2,184 cm^2, TA=3,864 cm^2

G070. $\dfrac{\sqrt{\pi}}{2}$

G071. 5

G072. 24 inches

G073. $\dfrac{25}{36}$

G074. 6 in

G075. 8 in & $8\sqrt{3}$ in

G076. $162\sqrt{3}$ ft^2

G077. $m\angle A = 88, m\angle B = 74, m\angle C = 92, m\angle D = 106$

G078. $\dfrac{1}{6}$

G079. $100\pi - 192$ m^2

G080. 126 units^2

G081. 170 in

G082. 37

G083. 11

G084. $m\angle A = 88, m\angle B = 74$

G085. 24 in

G086. 240 m^2

G087. 100 in^2

G088. LA=40π cm^2, TA=90π cm^2, V=100π cm^3

G089. 70 units^2

G090. $36\sqrt{3}$ ft^2

G091. 3 cm

G092. 1200 cm^3

G093. 40%

G094. $18\sqrt{2}$ cm^2

G095. $75\sqrt{3}$ cm^2

G096. 41 cm^2

G097. 69%

G098. 450 in^2

G099. 200 m^2

G100. XZ = 27, YZ = 36

G101. 60 liters

G102. 63 ft^2

G103. 44

G104. 108 in^3

G105. $4\pi - 3\sqrt{3}$ cm^2

G106. 2,500 ft^2

G107. cone, 2,000π cm^3

G108. 4 cm

G109. 792 in^2

G110. 8 feet

G111. $22\sqrt{2}, 11\sqrt{6}$

G112. $\sqrt{61}$ in, 117 in^2 OR $\sqrt{65}$ in, 118 in^2

G113. 2,601 ft^2

G114. 88 ft

G115. 34 ft

G116. 42 ft

G117. cylinder

G118. 1,089 cm^2

G119. 19

G120. 4 m

G121. $24\sqrt{3}$ in^2

G122. 136 ft^2

G123. 23

G124. 35 m

G125. 192 m^2

G126. 22 in

G127. 85 ft^2

G128. LA = 48m^2, TA = 84m^2

G129. 5m X 7m

G130. 242 units, 44 units

G131. 2x + 2y

G132. 15°

G133. 99 in^2

G134. 24 cm

G135. $LA = 780 cm^2$, $TA = 1180 cm^2$
$V = 2600 cm^3$

G136. 2 ft

G137. 2,520π mm^3

G138. 56 cm

G139. 200 liters

G140. $AC = 11$, $m\angle A = 60$, $BC = 11\sqrt{3}$
$m\angle D = m\angle E = 45$, $DE = 11\sqrt{2}$

G141. 16π

G142. 90 cm^2

G143. 130°

G144. 170°

G145. 100° & 148°

G146. 168 cm^2

G147. 45°

G148. 4,913 in^3

G149. 240 m^2

G150. 180 in^2

G151. 9 yards

G152. 48°, 57°, 123°

G153. 15

G154. volume is 12 times larger

G155. 160 ft^2

G156. $2\sqrt{41}$

G157. 6, 314, 50

G158. 288 tiles

G159. 75°

G160. 12

G161. 144 ft

G162. LA = 320 m^2, TA = 576 m^2

G163. 800 in^2

G164. $5\sqrt{5}$

G165. 60°

G166. $4\sqrt{6}$ m

G167. 64 cm^2

G168. 126 units^2

G169. 20

G170. 876 ft^2

G171. 648 cm^2

G172. 4% change in area

G173. 672 cm^2

G174. 9 inches

G175. 64 in^2

G176. 5

G177. 6

G178. 144 ft

G179. 11

G180. 20 m^2

G181. 30 inches

G182. 8

G183. 146 cm, 34 cm

G184. the area increased by 4%

G185. 12 cm^2

G186. x = 160°, y = z = 100°

G187. 675 cm^3

G188. 640 ft^2

G189. 248

G190. the square by 5 m^2

G191. 1980°

G192. $3\sqrt{555}$

G193. $13 \times \dfrac{13}{3}$ or 15×5

G194. $l = \dfrac{1}{3}p$

G195. 14 inches

G196. 53°

G197. 400 in^2

G198. 30°

G199. 48°, 57°, 57°, 123°

G200. $18\sqrt{2}$ cm

G201. increased by 4%

G202. 34 ft

G203. 156°

G204. 434

G205. $29.88

G206. 9.80 m

G207. 56 cm^2

G208. dimes

G209. 4 yards

G210. $787.50

G211. LA = 2,184 m^2, TA = 3,864 m^2

G212. LA = 480 m^2, TA = 736 m^2

G213. 9, 27

G214. 198 cm^2

G215. 1:2

G216. 64 cm^3

G217. the 19 inch pizza

G218. 225 ft^2

G219. 70 units^2

G220. $y = \dfrac{2}{3}x + 5$

G221. 69.4%

G222. x = 34, y = 112

G223. 24

G224. 198 cm^2

G225. 240 units^2

G226. 147.8 units^2

G227. LA = 90π cm^2, TA = 140π cm^2

G228. 81 m^3

G229. 12, 15, 12

G230. (208 − 52π) cm^2

G231. 1,980°

G232. 130°

G233. 960 units^2

G234. rhombus=419.2, square=400, rectangle=384

G235. 2200π cm^3

G236. x=100°, y=120°, z=140°, w=160°

G237. 120 m^2

G238. 48 ft^2

G239. 45°

G240. 1,920 cm^2

G241. 156°

G242. 35°, 85°

G243. 8 cm

G244. 60°, 80°, 100°, 120°

G245. $m\angle M = 35, m\angle P = 25, m\angle Q = 35$
$m\angle R = 120$, LM = 5, QR = 6

G246. 4,225 ft^2

G247. 32°, 148°

G248. 8

G249. 1:2

G250. 300 inches

G251. 9

G252. x = 9, y = 20

G253. r = h = 5m, V = 125π m^3

G254. 8

G255. $P = 3\sqrt{3}$ cm, $A = \dfrac{3\sqrt{3}}{4}$ cm^2

G256. 2,560π ft^3

G257. x = 10, y = 130

G258. LA = 780m^2, TA = 1180 m^2, V = 2600 m^3

G259. 8 ft^2

PROBABILITY AND STATISTICS ANSWERS

P001. 11

P002. $\dfrac{1}{9}$

P003. $\dfrac{5}{18}$

P004. 41

P005. $\dfrac{1}{2}$

P006. $\dfrac{3}{8}$

P007. 5

P008. $\dfrac{4}{13}$

P009. $66\dfrac{2}{3}\%$

P010. $\dfrac{2}{9}$

P011. 0.45

P012. 51

P013. 1.8

P014. 87

P015. 96

P016. $\dfrac{5}{9}$

P017. $\dfrac{1}{2}$

P018. $\dfrac{183}{200}$

P019. $\dfrac{7}{32}$

P020. 81

P021. $\dfrac{5}{12}$

P022. $\dfrac{1}{24}$

P023. $\dfrac{5}{42}$

P024. $\dfrac{1}{4}$

P025. $\dfrac{1}{9}$

P026. $\dfrac{1}{12}$

P027. $\dfrac{100-25\pi}{100}$

P028. $\dfrac{1}{3}$

P029. 845

P030. $\dfrac{3}{8}$

P031. $\dfrac{5}{16}$

P032. $\dfrac{100\pi-96}{100\pi}$

P033. $\dfrac{15}{32}$

P034. 13

P035. 78

P036. $\dfrac{1}{4}$

P037. $\dfrac{6}{31}$

P038. 65

P039. 77

P040. 5,000.5

P041. including Jane, 25

P042. $\dfrac{4}{15}$

P043. 36

P044. increased by $375

P045. 45

P046. 9

P047. $\dfrac{13}{32}$

P048. $\dfrac{5}{48}$

P049. $\dfrac{5}{16}$

P050. 16

P051. $\dfrac{2}{9}$

P052. 45¢

P053. 0.36

P054. 2.5

P055. median = 3, mode = 9

P056. $\dfrac{100-25\pi}{100\pi}$

P057. 65

P058. $\dfrac{100\pi-192}{100\pi}$

P059. $\dfrac{9}{20}$

P060. $\dfrac{1}{4}$

P061. $\dfrac{1}{12}$

P062. $\dfrac{1}{6}$

P063. $\dfrac{7}{24}$

P064. $\dfrac{1}{4}$

P065. 50

P066. $\dfrac{1}{9}$

P067. 24

P068. $\dfrac{7}{12}$

Important Mathematical Terms and Expressions for the Elementary Education Major

The elementary education major should have an understanding of the following mathematical terms and expressions to successful complete the certification process for licensure as a K – 6 elementary public school/ private school teacher.

absolute value	complementary angles	equivalent fractions
acute angle	composite number	estimate
add	concave	evaluate
addend	cone	even number
addition	constant	exact value
adjacent angles	convex	example
alternate exterior angles	concentric	exponent
alternate interior angles	concept	expression
altitude	congruent	exterior angle
angle	coordinate	
answer	corresponding angles	factor
arc	counting number	factorial (!)
arithmetic sequence	cube	factoring
area	cube number	Fibonacci sequence
average	cube root	figure
axiom	curve	finite
axis	cylinder	FOIL method
		formula
bar chart	data	fraction
bar graph	decagon	function
billion	decahedron	Fundamental Theorem of Arithmetic
binary	decimal	
binary operation	degree	geometric sequence
bisect	denominator	geometry
Box and Whisker Plot	diagram	graph
	Diameter	greatest common factor
calculate	difference	greater than (>)
cardinal number	digit	grid
cardinality	dimension	
cartesian coordinate system	discount	half
centimeter	discover	hemisphere
central angle	distance	hexagon
chance	divide	hexahedron
chart	divisibility	Hindu-Arabic Number System
chord	division	histogram
circle	dozen	horizontal
circular		hundredth
circumference	edge	hypotenuse
coefficient	element	
common denominator	equal	identity
common factor	equality	inch
common fraction	equation	inclination
common multiple	equilateral	inclusive
compass	equivalent	inequality

Infinite
Infinity
Inscribed angle
Integer
Interest
Interior angle
Intersect
Intersection
Interval
Inverse
Irrational number
Isosceles triangle

kilogram
kilometer

lateral side
lateral area
least common multiple
length
less than (<)

linear
line
line segment
liter
long division
lowest common denominator

major arc
margin
mean
measure
median
meter
midpoint
minor arc
mile
million
minus
mixed number
mode
model
multiple
multiplicand
multiplication
multiply

natural number
negative
notation
null set
number
number line
number pattern
numerator
numeral
numeric

object
Oblique
obtuse angle
obtuse triangle
octagon
octahedron
odd number
operation
order of operation
ordinal

origin
outcome
oval

palimage
parabola
parallel
parallelepiped
parallelogram
parentheses
partition
pattern
pentagon
percent
percentage
perimeter
perfect number
perpendicular
pi (π)
place value
plane
plot
plus
point
polyhedron

polygon
polynomial
portion
position
positive
power
practice
predict
prime
prime number
principle
prism
probability
problem
procedure
process
product
profit
proper fraction
properties
proportion
pyramid
Pythagorean Theorem

quadrant
quadratic
quadrilateral
quantity
quartiles
question
quotient

radical
radicand
radius
random
range
rank
rate
ratio
rational expression
rational number
ray
real number
reasoning
reciprocal
record

recursive
rectangle
rectangular
regular (polygon)
relationship
repeating decimal
repetition
replacement
remainder
right angle
right triangle
rhombus
root
rounded
rotation
rule

sales tax
sample space
scale
scale drawing
scalene
scientific notation
secant line
second
sector
segment
semicircle
semi prime
series
sequence
set
shape
significant
similar
simultaneous equations
single
slant height
slope
solid
skill
solution
solve
spatial
sphere
square
square root

squared
statistics
stem-and-leaf plot
straight angle
strategy
subset
substitution
subtraction
sum
supplement
supplementary angles
survey
symbols
symmetry
system of equations

tangent
tenth
terminating decimal
tetrahedron
theorem
theory
three-dimension
thousandth
total
times
trapezoid
triangle
triangular prism
trillion
trinomial
trisect

unary operation
union
unit
unit fraction
universal set
unknown

valid
value
variable
velocity
Venn diagram
vertex
vertical

vertical angles
volume

weight
whole number
width
work

x-axis
x-coordinate
x-intercept

y-axis
y-coordinate
y-intercept
yard

zero
zero (of a function)

About the author

Joseph Caruso was a K – 12 mathematic coordinators for the Somerville, MA public schools, serving in that position for 28 years. Upon retirement from that position, he was contacted to serve as an adjunct professor in the mathematics Department at Framingham State University, Framingham, MA, and he has been in that position to the present day.

The Association of Teachers of Mathematics in Massachusetts (ATMIM); the Association of Teachers of Mathematics in New England (ATMNE); the National Council of Teachers of Mathematics (NCTM); the National Council of Supervisors of Mathematics (NCSM); and the American Regions Mathematics League (ARML) are professional organizations that Joseph Caruso has been associated with.

Joseph Caruso has been involved in the preparation and supervision of students teachers at the following Massachusetts universities: Tufts University, Boston University, Simmons University, and Framingham State University.

In 2002, Joseph Caruso was selected to the Massachusetts Mathematics Educators Hall of Fame.

THE MATHEMATICS TUNER

FOR

ELEMENTARY EDUCATORS

Solve: $3^{2x-1} = 1$

What is the unit's digit of $2^{93} + 3^{91}$?

Find the area of a square with diagonal of length d.

A pair of dice are rolled. What is the probability of rolling a composite number?

www.ingramcontent.com/pod-product-compliance
Lightning Source LLC
Chambersburg PA
CBHW060603120726
48002CB00010B/2808